Mike McGrath

Assembly x64 Programming

In easy steps is an imprint of In Easy Steps Limited
16 Hamilton Terrace · Holly Walk · Leamington Spa
Warwickshire · United Kingdom · CV32 4LY
www.ineasysteps.com

Notice of Liability
Every effort has been made to ensure that this book contains accurate
and current information. However, In Easy Steps Limited and the
author shall not be liable for any loss or damage suffered by readers
as a result of any information contained herein.

Trademarks
All trademarks are acknowledged as belonging to their respective
companies.

In Easy Steps Limited supports The Forest Stewardship Council (FSC),
the leading international forest certification organization. All our titles
that are printed on Greenpeace approved FSC certified paper carry the
FSC logo.

MIX
Paper from
responsible sources
FSC® C020837

Printed and bound in the United Kingdom

ISBN 978-1-84078-952-2

Contents

How to Use This Book

The examples in this book demonstrate features of the Intel/AMD x64 Assembly programming language, and the screenshots illustrate the actual results produced by the listed code examples. The examples are created for the Microsoft Macro Assembler (MASM) that is included with the free Visual Studio Community Edition IDE. Certain colorization conventions are used to clarify the code listed in the book's easy steps...

Assembly directives and instructions are colored blue, register names are purple, labels and function names are red, literal text and numeric values are black, and code comments are green:

```
INCLUDELIB kernel32.lib    ; Import a library.
ExitProcess PROTO          ; Define an imported function.

.CODE                      ; Start of the code section.
main PROC                  ; Start of the main procedure.
XOR RCX, RCX               ; Clear a register.
MOV RCX, 10                ; Initialize a counter.
CALL ExitProcess           ; Return control to the system.
main ENDP                  ; End of the main procedure.
END                        ; End of the program.
```

To identify the source code for the example programs described in the steps, an icon and project name appear in the margin alongside the steps:

SIMD

Grab the Source Code
For convenience, the source code files from all examples featured in this book are available in a single ZIP archive. You can obtain this archive by following these easy steps:

1. Browse to **www.ineasysteps.com** then navigate to Free Resources and choose the Downloads section

2. Next, find Assembly x64 Programming in easy steps in the list, then click on the hyperlink entitled All Code Examples to download the ZIP archive file

3. Now, extract the archive contents to any convenient location on your computer

4. Each **Source.asm file** can be added to a Visual Studio project to run the code

If you don't achieve the result illustrated in any example, simply compare your code to that in the original example files you have downloaded to discover where you went wrong.

1 Beginning Basics

Welcome to the exciting world of Assembly programming. This chapter describes the Assembly language, computer architecture, and data representation.

Introducing Assembly

Assembly (ASM) is a low-level programming language for a computer or other programmable device. Unlike high-level programming languages such as C++, which are typically portable across different systems, the Assembly language targets a specific system architecture. This book demonstrates Assembly programming for the x86-64 computer system architecture – also known as "x64", "Intel64" and "AMD64".

Assembly language code is converted into machine instructions by an "assembler" utility program. There are several assemblers available but this book uses only the Microsoft Macro Assembler (MASM) on the Windows operating system.

The Assembly example programs in this book are created and tested in the free Community Edition of the Microsoft Visual Studio Integrated Development Environment (IDE).

At the heart of every computer is a microprocessor chip called the Central Processing Unit (CPU) that handles system operations, such as receiving input from the keyboard and displaying output on the screen. The CPU only understands "machine language instructions". These are binary strings of ones and zeros, which are in themselves too obscure for program development. The Assembly language overcomes this difficulty by providing symbols that represent machine language instructions in a useful format. Assembly is, therefore, also known as symbolic machine code.

Why learn Assembly language?
By learning Assembly you will discover...

- How the CPU accesses and executes instructions.

- How data is represented in computer memory.

- How instructions access and process data.

- How programs interface with the operating system.

- How to debug a high-level program with disassembly.

- How to handle memory addresses and pointers.

- How to create fast programs that require less memory.

Hot tip

Assembly is the only programming language that speaks directly to the computer's CPU.

Assembling and Linking

Creation of an executable program from Assembly source code is a two-stage process that requires the assembler to first create an object file, containing actual machine code, then a "linker" to incorporate any required library code and produce the executable.

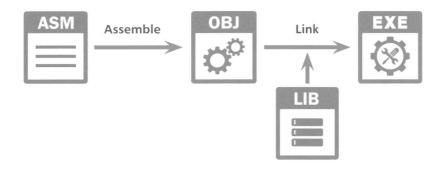

The 64-bit Microsoft Macro Assembler is a utility program named **ml64.exe** and the Microsoft Incremental Linker is a utility program named **link.exe**. Assembling and linking can be performed on the command line in a directory folder containing the Assembly source code file and both utility programs. The command must specify an Assembly source code file name to the **ml64** program, then call the linker with **/link**. Additionally, it must specify a **/subsystem:** execution mode (**console** or **windows**) and an **/entry:** point – the name of the first procedure to be executed in the Assembly code. The program can then be executed by name. For example, from an Assembly source code file named **hello.asm** with a **main** procedure:

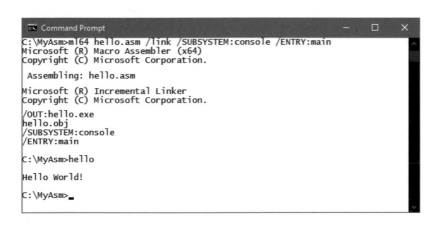

Assembling and linking is performed automatically when using the Visual Studio IDE, but the command line option is described here only to demonstrate the process. All examples in this book will be created and executed in the Visual Studio IDE.

You can find the source code of this program listed on page 154.

6

Inspecting Architecture

The fundamental design of nearly all computer systems is based upon a 1945 description by the eminent mathematician John von Neumann. The "von Neumann architecture" describes a computer design containing these components:

- **Processing unit** – containing an arithmetic logic unit and processor registers.

- **Control unit** – containing an instruction register and program counter.

- **Memory** – in which to store data and instructions.

- **External mass storage** – hard disk drive/solid state drive.

- **Input and Output mechanisms** – keyboard, mouse, etc.

Today's computers have a CPU (combining the control unit, arithmetic logic unit, and processor registers), main memory (Random Access Memory – "RAM"), external mass storage (Hard Disk Drive "HDD" or Solid State Drive "SSD"), and various I/O devices for input and output. These components are all connected by the "system bus", which allows data, address, and control signals to transfer between the components.

Computer system architecture defined by the Hungarian-American mathematician John von Neumann (1903-1957).

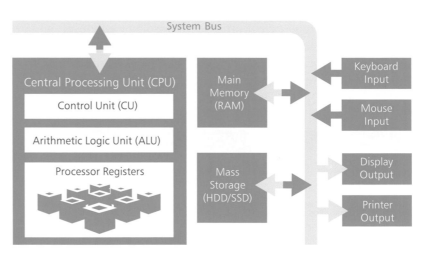

The CPU is the "brain" of the computer. A program is loaded into memory, then the CPU gets instructions from memory and executes them. Accessing memory is slow though, so the CPU contains registers in which to store data that it can access quickly.

...cont'd

The control unit can decode and execute instructions fetched from memory, and direct the operations of the CPU. The arithmetic logic unit performs arithmetic operations, such as addition and subtraction, plus logical operations, such as **AND** and **OR**. This means that all data processing is done within the CPU.

Logical operations are described and demonstrated later – see page 18.

The conceptual view of main memory shown below consists of rows of blocks. Each block is called a "bit" and can store a 0 or 1. The right-most bit (**0**) is called the "Least Significant Bit" (LSB) and the left-most bit (**7**) is called the "Most Significant Bit" (MSB).

	MSB							LSB	
Address	7	6	5	4	3	2	1	0	
00000000	1	0	0	1	1	0	0	1	← Byte
00000001	1	1	0	1	1	0	1	1	
00000002	0	1	0	0	1	0	1	0	
00000003	0	1	0	1	0	1	0	1	
00000004	1	0	1	0	0	1	1	0	
00000005	0	0	1	1	0	1	1	1	
00000006	1	0	1	0	1	1	0	1	
00000007	1	1	0	0	1	0	0	0	← Bit

As a bit can only store 0 or 1, a group of bits can be used to represent larger numbers. For example, two bits can represent numbers 0-3, three bits can represent numbers 0-7, and so on.

Data allocation directives defines these groups of bits in Assembly:

- **BYTE** – Byte (8-bits) range 0-255, or -128 to 127

- **WORD** – Word (16-bits) range 0-65,535, or -32,768 to 32,767

- **DWORD** – Double word (32-bits) range $0-2^{32}$, or -2^{31} to $2^{31}-1$

- **QWORD** – Quad word (64-bits) range $0-2^{64}$, or -2^{63} to $2^{63}-1$

Consecutive addresses are allocated for groups of bits that contain multiple bytes, and their content is accessed via the memory address of the first byte.

Each row in the view above is a byte – usually the smallest addressable unit of memory. Each byte has a unique address by which you can access its content – for example, to access the content of the third row here via address **00000002**.

Addressing Registers

Although an x86-64 CPU has many registers, it includes 16 general-purpose 64-bit user-accessible registers that are of special significance in Assembly programming. The first eight of these are extensions of eight registers from the earlier Intel 8086 microprocessor, and are addressed in Assembly programming by their historic names **RAX**, **RBX**, **RCX**, **RDX**, **RSI**, **RDI**, **RBP** and **RSP**. The rest are addressed as **R8**, **R9**, **R10**, **R11**, **R12**, **R13**, **R14** and **R15**.

Low-order (right-side) byte, word, and double word fractions of the 64-bit registers can be addressed individually. For example, **AL** (low byte) and **AH** (high byte), **AX** (word) and **EAX** (double word) are all fractions of the **RAX** register.

64-bit	32-bit	16-bit	8-bit
RAX	EAX	AX	AH AL
RBX	EBX	BX	BH BL
RCX	ECX	CX	CH CL
RDX	EDX	DX	DH DL
RSI	ESI	SI	SIL
RDI	EDI	DI	DIL
RBP	EBP	BP	BPL
RSP	ESP	SP	SPL
R8	R8D	R8W	R8B
R9	R9D	R9W	R9B
R10	R10D	R10W	R10B
R11	R11D	R11W	R11B
R12	R12D	R12W	R12B
R13	R13D	R13W	R13B
R14	R14D	R14W	R14B
R15	R15D	R15W	R15B

Don't forget

Storing a value in the smaller fractional parts of a 64-bit register does not affect the higher bits, but storing a value in a 32-bit register will fill the top of the 64-bit register with zeros.

RAX			
	EAX		
		AX	
		AH	AL

...cont'd

The **RSP** and **RBP** 64-bit registers are used for stack operations and stack frame operations, but all the other registers can be used for computation in your Assembly programs.

Some 64-bit registers serve an additional purpose – either directly on the CPU hardware or in the x64 Windows calling convention. When a function is called within an Assembly program, the caller may pass it a number of argument values that get assigned, in sequential order, to the **RCX**, **RDX**, **R8**, and **R9** registers.

A procedure will only save those values within non-volatile registers – those values within volatile registers may be lost.

Stack (RSP) and stack frame (RBP) operations are described later – see Chapter 7.

Register	Hardware	Calling Convention	Volatility
RAX	Accumulator	Function return value	Volatile
RBX	Base		Non-volatile
RCX	Counter	1st Function argument	Volatile
RDX	Data	2nd Function argument	Volatile
RSI	Source Index		Non-volatile
RDI	Destination Index		Non-volatile
RBP	Base Pointer		Non-volatile
RSP	Stack Pointer		Non-volatile
R8	General-purpose	3rd Function argument	Volatile
R9	General-purpose	4th Function argument	Volatile
R10	General-purpose		Volatile
R11	General-purpose		Volatile
R12	General-purpose		Non-volatile
R13	General-purpose		Non-volatile
R14	General-purpose		Non-volatile
R15	General-purpose		Non-volatile

One more 64-bit register to be aware of is the **RIP** instruction pointer register. This should not be used directly in your Assembly programs as it stores the address of the next instruction to execute. The CPU will execute the instruction at the address in the **RIP** register then increment the register to point to the next instruction.

Some Assembly instructions can modify the **RIP** instruction pointer address to make the program jump to a different location – see page 62.

Numbering Systems

64
40h
0010 0000b

Numeric values in Assembly program code may appear in the familiar decimal format that is used in everyday life, but computers use the binary format to store the values. Binary numbers are lengthy strings of zeros and ones, which are difficult to read so the hexadecimal format is often used to represent binary data. Comparison of these three numbering systems is useful to understand how numeric values are represented in each system.

Decimal (base 10) – uses numbers 0-9.

Columns from right to left are the value 10 raised to the power of an incrementing number, starting at zero:

10^2	10^1	10^0
1	2	8

$$8 \times 10^0 = 8$$
$$2 \times 10^1 = 20 \ (2 \times 10)$$
$$1 \times 10^2 = \underline{100} \ (1 \times 10 \times 10)$$
$$\underline{128}$$

Binary (base 2) – uses numbers 0 and 1.

Columns from right to left are the value 2 raised to the power of an incrementing number, starting at zero:

```
 1   0   1   1   0   0   1   0
128  64  32  16   8   4   2   1
MSB                        LSB
```

2^3	2^2	2^1	2^0
1	0	0	1

$$1 \times 2^0 = 1$$
$$0 \times 2^1 = 0$$
$$0 \times 2^2 = 0$$
$$1 \times 2^3 = \underline{8} \ (1 \times 2 \times 2 \times 2)$$
$$\underline{9}$$

1001 binary = **9** decimal

Hexadecimal (base 16) – uses numbers 0-9 & letters A-F.

Columns from right to left are the value 16 raised to the power of an incrementing number, starting at zero:

16^2	16^1	16^0
2	3	F

$$15 \times 16^0 = 15$$
$$3 \times 16^1 = 48 \ (3 \times 16)$$
$$2 \times 16^2 = \underline{512} \ (2 \times 16 \times 16)$$
$$\underline{575}$$

23F hexadecimal = **575** decimal

Binary	Hex
0000	0
0001	1
0010	2
0011	3
0100	4
0101	5
0110	6
0111	7
1000	8
1001	9
1010	A
1011	B
1100	C
1101	D
1110	E
1111	F

Converting Binary to Hexadecimal

The table on the left can be used to easily convert a value between binary and hexadecimal numbering systems.

Notice that each hexadecimal digit represents four binary digits. This means you can separate any binary number into groups of 4-bits from right to left, then substitute the appropriate hexadecimal digit for each group. If the left-most group has less than 4-bits just add leading zeros. For example:

11 1101 0101

becomes

0011 1101 0101

3   D   5

1111010101 binary = **3D5** hexadecimal

A 4-bit group is called a "nibble" (sometimes spelled as "nybble").

Similarly, you can use the table to convert each hexadecimal digit to the equivalent group of 4 binary digits to easily convert a value between hexadecimal and binary numbering systems.
For example:

6   C   4

0110 1100 0100

6C4 hexadecimal = **011011000100** binary

Denoting the Numbering System

When using numbers in your Assembly programs you must denote which numbering system they are using if not the decimal system. Add a **b** suffix to denote binary, or add an **h** suffix for hexadecimal.

Decimal: **21**
Binary: **00010101b**
Hexadecimal: **15h**

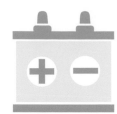

Signing Numbers

Binary numbers can represent unsigned positive numbers (zero is also considered positive) or signed positive and negative numbers. Page 15 describes the binary representation of unsigned numbers and their conversion to hexadecimal and decimal.

In representing signed numbers, the left-most Most Significant Bit (MSB) is used to denote whether the number is positive or negative. For positive numbers, this "sign bit" will contain a 0, whereas for negative numbers, the sign bit will contain a 1. This reduces the numeric range capacity of a bit group by one bit.

For any group of **N** number of bits, the maximum unsigned number is calculated as 2^N **-1**. For example, with a byte group (8-bits), the capacity is 2^8 **-1**, or **256 -1**, so the range is **0-255**.

Hot tip

Signed groups of bits in Assembly programming are defined as **SBYTE**, **SWORD**, and **SDWORD**.

1	1	1	1	1	1	1	1

= **255** decimal

But when the MSB is used as a sign bit, the maximum signed number is calculated as 2^{N-1} **-1**. For example, with a byte group (8-bits), the capacity is 2^{8-1} **-1**, which is 2^7 **-1** or **128 -1**, so the range is **0-127**.

Sign Bit ⟶

0	1	1	1	1	1	1	1

= **+127** decimal

Negative signed numbers are stored in binary as a "Two's Complement" representation. To convert this to a decimal number, the value in each bit (except the sign bit) must be inverted – so that **0**s become **1**s, and **1**s become **0**s. Then, add **1** to the Least Significant Bit (LSB) using binary arithmetic. Finally, observe the sign value denoted by the sign bit. For example:

Hot tip

You can use the Calculator app's Scientific options in Windows to calculate the result of raising to power values.

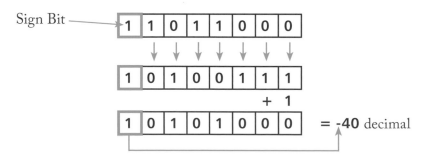

Storing Characters

Just as signed and unsigned decimal numbers can be stored in binary format, so too can alphanumeric characters. The American Standard Code for Information Interchange (ASCII) provides a unique code for individual characters. The basic ASCII standard supplies individual codes for 128 characters and these differentiate between uppercase and lowercase characters. Each code is a unique 7-bit number, so a byte is used to store each character. For example, the uppercase letter **A** has a decimal code of **65** (**41** hexadecimal) and is stored in a byte as the binary number **01000001**. The alphanumeric ASCII codes are listed below:

Decimal	Hex	Character	Decimal	Hex	Character
65	41	A	97	61	a
66	42	B	98	62	b
67	43	C	99	63	c
68	44	D	100	64	d
69	45	E	101	65	e
70	46	F	102	66	f
71	47	G	103	67	g
72	48	H	104	68	h
73	49	I	105	69	i
74	4A	J	106	6A	j
75	4B	K	107	6B	k
76	4C	L	108	6C	l
77	4D	M	109	6D	m
78	4E	N	110	6E	n
79	4F	O	111	6F	o
80	50	P	112	70	p
81	51	Q	113	71	q
82	52	R	114	72	r
83	53	S	115	73	s
84	54	T	116	74	t
85	55	U	117	75	u
86	56	V	118	76	v
87	57	W	119	77	w
88	58	X	120	78	x
89	59	Y	121	79	y
90	5A	Z	122	7A	z

There are ASCII codes for the numeral characters 0-9. The character 5, for example, is not the same as the number 5.

Decimal	Hex	Character
48	30	0
49	31	1
50	32	2
51	33	3
52	34	4
53	35	5
54	36	6
55	37	7
56	38	8
57	39	9

ASCII was later expanded to represent more characters in ANSI character code.

Using Boolean Logic

The CPU recognizes **AND**, **OR**, **XOR**, **TEST** and **NOT** instructions to perform boolean logic operations, which can be used in Assembly programming to set, clear, and test bit values. The syntax of these instructions looks like this:

AND	*Operand1* , *Operand2*
OR	*Operand1* , *Operand2*
XOR	*Operand1* , *Operand2*
TEST	*Operand1* , *Operand2*
NOT	*Operand1*

In all cases, the first operand can be either the name of a register or system memory, whereas the second operand can be the name of a register, system memory, or an immediate numeric value.

AND Operation

The **AND** operation compares two bits and returns a **1** only if <u>both</u> bits contain a value of **1** – otherwise it returns **0**. For example:

	Operand1:	**0101**
	Operand2:	**0011**
After **AND**...	Operand1:	**0001**

The **AND** operation can be used to check whether a number is odd or even by comparing the Least Significant Bit in the first operand to **0001**. If the LSB contains **1** the number is odd, otherwise the number is even.

OR Operation

The **OR** operation compares two bits and returns a **1** if either or both bits contain a **1** – if both are **0** it returns **0**. For example:

	Operand1:	**0101**
	Operand2:	**0011**
After **OR**...	Operand1:	**0111**

The **OR** operation can be used to set one or more bits by comparing the bit values in the first operand to selective bits containing a value of **1** in the second operand. This ensures that the selective bits will each return **1** in the result.

The term "boolean" refers to a system of logical thought developed by the English mathematician George Boole (1815-1864).

... **cont'd**

XOR Operation

The **XOR** (eXclusive OR) operation compares two bits and returns a **1** only if the bits contain different values – otherwise, if both are **1** or both are **0**, it returns **0**. For example:

	Operand1:	0101
	Operand2:	0011
After **XOR**...	Operand1:	0110

The **XOR** operation can be used to clear an entire register to zero by comparing all its bits to itself. In this case, all bits will match so the **XOR** operation returns a **0** in each bit of the register.

TEST Operation

The **TEST** operation works just like the **AND** operation, except it does not change the value in the first operand. Instead, the **TEST** operation sets a "zero flag" according to the result. For example:

	Operand1:	0101
	Operand2:	0011
After **TEST**...	Operand1:	0101 (unchanged)

The **TEST** operation can be used to check whether a number is odd or even by comparing the Least Significant Bit in the first operand to **0001**. If the number is even, the zero flag is **1**, but if the number is odd, the **TEST** operation sets the zero flag to **0**.

NOT Operation

The **NOT** operation inverts the value in each bit of a single operand – 1s become 0s, and 0s become 1s. For example:

	Operand1:	0011
After **NOT**...	Operand1:	1100

The **NOT** operation can be used to negate a signed binary number to a Two's Complement. The **NOT** operation will invert each bit value, then **1** can be added to the result to find the binary number's Two's Complement.

A comprehensive description and demonstration of flags is given on page 60.

19

Summary

- Assembly is a low-level programming language that targets a specific computer system architecture.

- The assembler creates an object file containing machine code, and the linker incorporates any required library code.

- An executable program can be created from Assembly source code on the command line or in the Visual Studio IDE.

- Most computer systems are based on the von Neumann architecture with CPU, memory, storage and I/O devices.

- The CPU contains a control unit, arithmetic logic unit, and processor registers in which to store data for fast access.

- A byte has eight bits that can each store a 0 or a 1, and each byte has a unique memory address to access its content.

- A word consists of two bytes, a double word consists of four bytes, and a quad word consists of eight bytes (64-bits)

- An x86-64 CPU has 16 user-accessible 64-bit registers that are used in Assembly programming.

- Low-order byte, word, and double word fractions of the 64-bit registers can be addressed individually.

- Some 64-bit registers have a special purpose, either on the CPU hardware or in the x64 Windows calling convention.

- On completion of a procedure, values in non-volatile registers are saved but values in volatile registers may not be saved.

- Numeric values in Assembly programming may appear in the decimal, hexadecimal, or binary numbering system.

- Conversion between binary and hexadecimal is performed by separating a binary number into groups of 4-bits.

- Signed numbers are stored in binary as a Two's Complement representation.

- Characters are stored in binary as their ASCII code value.

- The CPU provides **AND**, **OR**, **XOR**, **TEST** and **NOT** instructions to perform boolean logic operations.

2 Getting Started

Installing Visual Studio

Assembly 64-bit programming for Windows uses the Microsoft Macro Assembler (MASM) file **ml64.exe** and linker **link.exe**. These are included in a Microsoft Visual Studio installation when you choose to install Visual Studio for C++ development.

Microsoft Visual Studio is the professional development tool that provides a fully Integrated Development Environment (IDE) for many programming languages. For instance, within its IDE, code can be written in C++, C#, or the Visual Basic programming language to create Windows applications.

Visual Studio Community edition is a streamlined version of Visual Studio specially created for those people learning programming. It has a simplified user interface and omits advanced features of the professional edition to avoid confusion. Within its IDE for C++, code can also be written in the Assembly programming language to create applications.

The Visual Studio Community edition is completely free and can be installed on any system meeting the following minimum requirements:

Visual Studio is used to develop computer programs, web apps, mobile apps, and more.

Component	Requirement
Operating system	Windows 10 (version 1703 or higher) Windows Server 2019 Windows 8.1 (with update 2919355) Windows 7 Service Pack 1 Windows Server 2012 R2
CPU (processor)	1.8 GHz or faster
RAM (memory)	2 Gb (8 Gb recommended)
HDD (hard drive)	Up to 210 Gb available space
Video Card	Minimum resolution of 1280 x 720 Optimum resolution of 1366 x 768

The Visual Studio Community edition is used throughout this book to demonstrate programming with Assembly language, but the examples can also be recreated in Visual Studio. Follow the steps opposite to install the Visual Studio Community edition.

1 Open your web browser and navigate to the Visual Studio Community download page – at the time of writing this can be found at **visualstudio.microsoft.com/vs/community**

Installation of Visual Studio is handled by an installer application. You can re-run the installer at a later date to add or remove features.

2 Click the **Download Visual Studio** button to get the Visual Studio Installer

3 Open your **Downloads** folder, then click on the installer file icon to launch the installer's setup dialog

4 On the setup dialog, click the **Continue** button to fetch some setup files – on completion the Visual Studio Installer will appear

5 Select the **Workloads** tab, then choose the **C++** option as the type of installation

Choosing a different destination folder may require other paths to be adjusted later – it's simpler to just accept the suggested default.

6 Finally, to begin the download, click the **Install** button and wait until the installation process has completed

Exploring the IDE

1 Go to your apps menu, then select the Visual Studio menu item added there by the installer:

2 Sign in with your Microsoft account, or register an account then sign in to continue

3 See a default **Start Page** appear where recent projects will be listed alongside several "Get started" options

The first time Visual Studio starts it takes a few minutes as it performs configuration routines.

24

In the future, your recent projects will be listed here so you can easily reopen them.

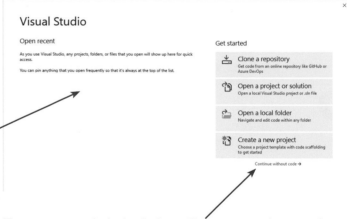

4 For now, just click the link to **Continue without code** to launch the Visual Studio application

The Visual Studio Integrated Development Environment (IDE) appears, from which you have instant access to everything needed to produce complete Windows applications – from here, you can create exciting visual interfaces, enter code, compile and execute applications, debug errors, and much more.

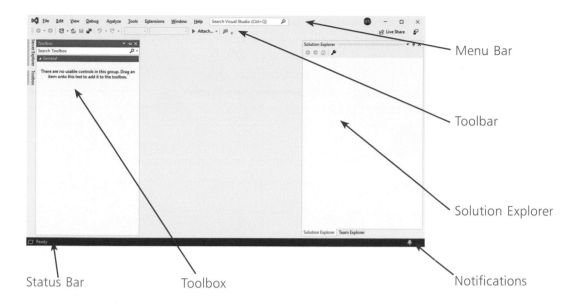

Menu Bar

Toolbar

Solution Explorer

Status Bar

Toolbox

Notifications

Visual Studio IDE components

The Visual Studio IDE initially provides these standard features:

- **Menu Bar** – where you can select actions to perform on all your project files and to access Help. When a project is open, extra menus of Project and Build are shown in addition to the default menu selection of File, Edit, View, Debug, Analyze, Tools, Extensions, Window, and Help.

- **Toolbar** – where you can perform the most popular menu actions with just a single click on its associated shortcut icon.

- **Toolbox** – where you can select visual elements to add to a project. Click the Toolbox side bar button to see its contents. When a project is open, "controls" such as Button, Label, CheckBox, RadioButton, and TextBox may be shown here.

- **Solution Explorer** – where you can see at a glance all the files and resource components contained within an open project.

- **Status Bar** – where you can read the state of the current activity being undertaken. When building an application, a "Build started" message is displayed here, changing to a "Build succeeded" or "Build failed" message upon completion.

Hot tip

To change the color, choose the **Tools**, **Options** menu then select **Environment**, **General, Color Theme**.

25

Creating a MASM Template

When you launch Visual Studio, the "Get started" options listed on the Start Page include a **Create New Project** option that allows you to begin a project by selecting one of a number of existing preconfigured templates. There is no preconfigured project template for Assembly code, but you can create your own template for Assembly by reconfiguring an existing template:

1 Launch Visual Studio, then select **Create a new project** to see a scrollable list of template options appear

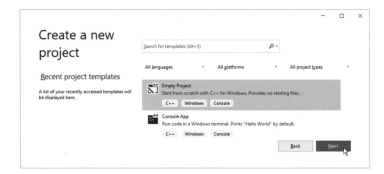

2 Select the **Empty Project** with C++ for Windows option, then click the **Next** button to open a configuration dialog

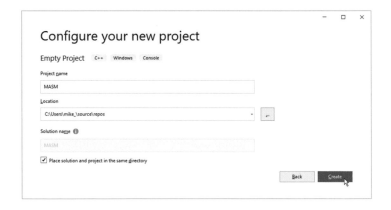

3 Type "MASM" (without the quote marks) into the **Project Name** box, accept the suggested location options and click the **Create** button – to create the project and see the Visual Studio IDE appear

4 Select **View**, **Solution Explorer** – to open a "Solution Explorer" window, displaying the project's contents

5 In Solution Explorer, delete the unrequired folders for **Header Files**, **Resource Files** and **Source Files**

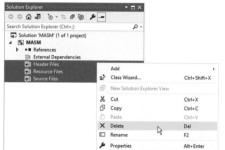

Hot tip

The **Solution Explorer** window may already be visible when the Visual Studio IDE appears.

6 Next, in Solution Explorer, right-click on the project name icon (MASM) to open a context menu

7 From the menu, choose **Build Dependencies**, then **Build Customizations...** – to open a "Visual C++ Build Customization Files" dialog

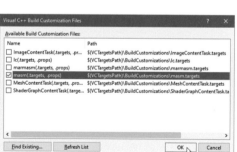

8 In the dialog, check the **masm(.targets, .props)** item, then click the **OK** button to close the dialog

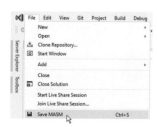

9 On the Visual Studio main menu, click **File**, **Save MASM** to save the changes you have made so far – additional changes will be made on pages 28-29 to configure the linker and add a "barebones" Assembly (**.asm**) source file

Configuring the Linker

Continuing the creation of a template for Assembly code from pages 26-27, a SubSystem and code Entry Point can be specified for the linker in this project:

1 On the Visual Studio toolbar, set the platform to **x64** – for 64-bit Assembly code

2 Then, on the main menu, select **Project, Properties** to open a "Property Pages" dialog

3 Set the Configuration option to **All Configurations** and the Platform option to **x64**

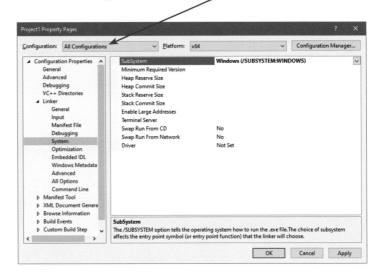

Hot tip

Choosing Windows as the SubSystem prevents a Console window appearing whenever a project executes. You can change the SubSystem to Console if you need to see output or input via the command line in a particular project.

4 Expand **Configuration Properties, Linker** in the left pane, then select the **System** item

5 In the right pane, select **SubSystem**, then click the arrow button and choose the **Windows (SUBSYSTEM:WINDOWS)** option from the drop-down list that appears

6 Click the **Apply** button to save this setting

7 Now, select **Linker**, **Advanced** in the left pane

8 In the right pane, select **Entry Point,** then type "main" (without the quote marks)

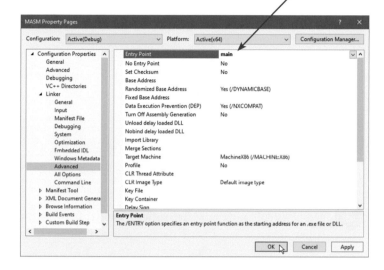

The "main" Entry Point is the name of the first procedure to be executed when a program runs. The procedure named "main" will appear as the first procedure in a barebones Assembly source file that will be added next.

9 Click the **Apply** button to save this setting

10 Click the **OK** button to close the dialog

11 On the Visual Studio main menu, click **File**, **Save MASM** to save the changes you have made so far – additional changes will be made on the next page to add a "barebones" Assembly (**.asm**) source file

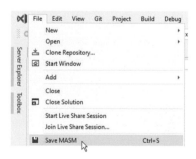

Adding a Source Code File

Continuing the creation of a template for Assembly code from pages 28-29, a barebones source code file can be added in which you can write Assembly language instructions:

1 In Solution Explorer, right-click on the project MASM icon to open a context menu, then choose **Add**, **New Item** – to open an "Add New Item" dialog

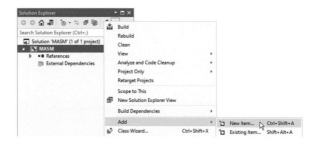

2 In the dialog, expand **Installed**, **Visual C++** in the left pane, then select **C++ File** in the right pane

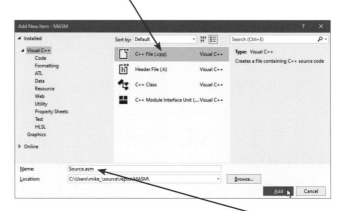

3 Now, change the "Name" from **Source.cpp** to **Source.asm** then click the **Add** button to close the dialog

4 See a **Source.asm** icon appear in Solution Explorer – double-click this icon to open the file in the text editor window, ready to receive Assembly code

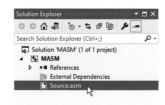

...cont'd

5 In the text editor, precisely type this barebones code

```
INCLUDELIB kernel32.lib  ; Import a standard Windows library.
ExitProcess PROTO        ; Define an imported library function.

.DATA                    ; Start of the data section.
                         ; <- Variable declarations go here.

.CODE                    ; Start of the code section.
main PROC                ; Program entry procedure.
                         ; <- Assembly instructions go here.
CALL ExitProcess         ; Execute the imported library function.
main ENDP                ; End of the main procedure.

END                      ; End of the Assembly program.
```

In Assembly language, code comments begin with a semi-colon – the compiler ignores everything after a semi-colon on a line. Comments are important in Assembly source code to explain the program to other developers, or to yourself when revisiting the code later. Comments are mostly omitted from the code listed in this book due to space limitations, but are included in the source code you can download (see page 7).

6 On the Visual Studio toolbar, choose **x64** and click **File**,

Save All to save changes, then click the **Local Windows Debugger** button to assemble and run the code – it should execute without errors

7 From the main menu, select **Project**, **Export Template** to launch the "Export Template Wizard" dialog

8 In the dialog, select **Project Template**, then click the **Next** button

9 Now, enter **Template Name** "MASM" and a **Template Description**, then click the **Finish** button to close the dialog

10 On the main menu, click **File**, **Close Solution**, then click **Create a new project** on the Start Page to see the MASM template has been added to the listed templates

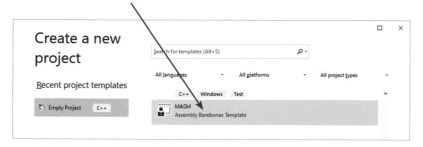

The **kernel32.lib** library provides an **ExitProcess** function that returns control to Windows after execution of Assembly instructions.

Moving Data into Storage

Having created a template for Assembly code on pages 26-31, you can now create a simple project to store items in the CPU registers and in system memory (RAM) variables.

The basic key Assembly **MOV** instruction is used to assign (copy) data to a register or to a memory variable. The **MOV** instruction requires two "operands" and has this syntax:

MOV *Destination* **,** *Source*

- **Destination** – a register name, or a memory variable.

- **Source** – a register name, a memory variable, or an "immediate" operand – typically a numeric value.

It is important to recognize that both operands must be of the same size. Assigning a variable to a 64-bit register therefore requires the variable to be 64 bits in size – a quad word.

Variables must be declared in the data section of the Assembly code by specifying a name of your choice, the data allocation size, and an initial value, with this syntax:

Variable-name   *Data-allocation*   *Initial-value*

Variable Naming Convention
The variable name can begin with any letter **A-Z** (in uppercase or lowercase) or any of the characters **@_$?**. The remainder of the name can contain any of those characters and numbers **0-9**. Variable names throughout this book are lowercase, to easily distinguish them from the register names in all uppercase.

Variable Data Allocation
The directive keyword **QWORD** can be used to allocate 64 bits of storage for each initial variable value. This allows the variable value to be easily assigned to a 64-bit register, and for the value in a 64-bit register to be easily assigned to a variable. The same data allocation can be specified using **DQ** (a synonym for **QWORD**), but the **QWORD** directive is preferred throughout this book for clarity.

Variable Initialization
An initial value is typically specified in the variable declaration, but can be replaced by a **?** question mark character if the variable is to be initialized later in the program.

Beware

The maximum length of a variable name is 247 characters.

32

...cont'd

1 Launch Visual Studio, then select **Create a new project** and choose the **MASM Template** you created previously

MOV

2 Name the project "MOV" (without the quote marks)

3 Open the **Source.asm** file in the editor window

4 In the .**DATA** section of the file, add the following line of code to create a 64-bit variable that contains an initial integer value of 100
var QWORD 100   ; Initialize variable mem.

5 In the .**CODE** section **main** procedure (immediately below the line containing **main PROC**), insert two lines of code to clear two 64-bit registers to zero
XOR RCX, RCX   ; Clear reg.
XOR RDX, RDX   ; Clear reg.

See page 19 to discover how the eXclusive OR (XOR) instruction **XOR** clears a register to zero.

6 Next, assign an immediate value to the first clear register
MOV RCX, 33   ; Assign reg/imm.

7 Assign the value in the first register to the second register
MOV RDX, RCX   ; Assign reg/reg.

8 Now, assign the value contained in the variable to the first register
MOV RCX, var   ; Assign reg/mem.

9 Assign the value in the second register to the variable
MOV var, RDX   ; Assign mem/reg.

10 On the main Visual Studio menu, click the **File**, **Save Source.asm** options to save the code

If an error message appears, check you have selected x64 on the Visual Studio toolbar then carefully check your code to find the mistake.

11 Choose **x64** on the toolbar and click the **Local Windows Debugger** button to run the code

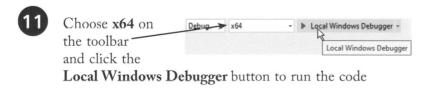

Stepping into Instructions

Having created a simple project for Assembly code on pages 32-33, you can now run the program line-by-line by setting an initial "breakpoint" that halts execution of the program, so you can then "step into" each individual line of code.

Visual Studio provides two Debug Windows that allow you to inspect how each Assembly instruction affects the CPU registers and system memory variables:

1 In Visual Studio, open the "MOV" project, created on pages 32-33, then open its **Source.asm** file in the editor

Click a red dot marking a breakpoint to remove that breakpoint.

2 Click in the gray margin to the left of the first **MOV** instruction to set a breakpoint at that line – see a red dot appear there, marking the breakpoint

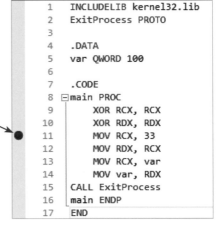

```
Source.asm  ⊣ ×
     1      INCLUDELIB kernel32.lib
     2      ExitProcess PROTO
     3
     4      .DATA
     5      var QWORD 100
     6
     7      .CODE
     8  ⊟main PROC
     9          XOR RCX, RCX
    10          XOR RDX, RDX
    11          MOV RCX, 33
    12          MOV RDX, RCX
    13          MOV RCX, var
    14          MOV var, RDX
    15      CALL ExitProcess
    16      main ENDP
    17      END
```

3 On the menu bar, click **Debug**, **Options** – to open an "Options" dialog

4 Select **Debugging** in the left pane, ensure that **Enable address-level debugging** is checked in the right pane, and click the **OK** button to close the dialog

The Registers window will not be available unless address-level debugging is enabled. Click **Debug**, **Options**, **Debugging**, **General** then check **Enable address-level debugging**.

5 On the toolbar, click the **Local Windows Debugger** button to run the code – see execution halt at the breakpoint

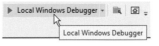

6 Now, click **Debug**, **Windows**, **Registers** – to see the current CPU register values in hexadecimal format

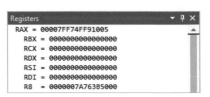

```
Registers                              ⊣ ¤ ×
RAX = 00007FF74FF91005
 RBX = 0000000000000000
 RCX = 0000000000000000
 RDX = 0000000000000000
 RSI = 0000000000000000
 RDI = 0000000000000000
 R8  = 0000007A763B5000
```

...cont'd

7 Next, click **Debug**, **Windows**, **Watch**, **Watch 1** – to open a "Watch" window

8 In the Watch window, click the **Add item to watch** panel then, in turn add the **var**, **RCX** and **RDX** items

XOR RCX, RCX

XOR RDX, RDX

9 On the toolbar, click the **Step Into** button once to execute the instruction after the breakpoint

Step Into (F11)

10 Examine the Registers window and Watch window to see a value has been moved into a CPU register

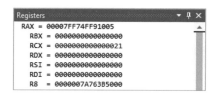

MOV RCX, 33

11 Repeat Steps 9 and 10 to see values moved between CPU registers and between system memory until the end of the program is reached, then click **Debug**, **Stop Debugging**

MOV RDX, RCX

MOV RCX, var

MOV var, RDX

Fixing Constant Values

In addition to variable declarations, the **.DATA** section of an Assembly program can declare constants. Constant declarations do not use system memory, but insert their literal values directly into the Assembly code. Unlike variable declarations, constant declarations must specify the value to be stored, and this is a fixed value that cannot be changed during execution of the program.

Declaration of a constant requires the **EQU** ("equates to") directive be used to specify a value to be assigned to a constant name of your choice – following the same naming convention as for variables. The syntax of a constant declaration looks like this:

Constant-name	**EQU**	*Fixed-value*

The value stored in a constant can be assigned to a register with the **MOV** instruction, but you cannot assign a value to a constant using a **MOV** instruction. You can, however, use a constant value in an expression together with the following numeric operators:

Operator	Operation
+	Addition
-	Subtraction
*	Multiplication
/	Integer division
MOD	Modulus (remainder)

Hot tip

Variable names can also be used with numeric operators in expressions.

For expressions containing more than one numeric operator it is important to recognize that the multiplication, division, and modulus operators take precedence over the addition and subtraction operators. This means that operations with higher precedence are performed before those of lower precedence. This can lead to undesirable results, but the default precedence can be overridden by using parentheses to determine the order of operation. Operations enclosed in the innermost parentheses will be performed before those in outer parentheses. For example, the expression **1 + 5 * 3** evaluates to 16, not 18, because the ***** multiplication operator has a higher precedence than the **+** addition operator. Parentheses can be used to specify precedence, so that **(1 + 5) * 3** evaluates to 18 because the addition now gets performed before the multiplication operation.

1. Launch Visual Studio, then select **Create a new project** and choose the **MASM Template** you created previously

ASM

EQU

2. Name the project "EQU" (without the quote marks), then open the **Source.asm** file in the editor window

3. In the .**DATA** section of the file, add the following line to create a constant that contains a fixed value of 12
   con EQU 12   ; *Initialize constant mem.*

4. In the .**CODE main** procedure, insert instructions to assign to two registers using the constant value in expressions
   MOV RCX, con   ; *Assign reg/mem.*
   MOV RDX, con + 8   ; *Assign reg/mem + imm.*
   MOV RCX, con + 8 * 2   ; *Assign unclear expr.*
   MOV RDX, (con + 8) * 2   ; *Assign clear expr.*
   MOV RCX, con MOD 5   ; *Assign modulo quotient.*
   MOV RDX, (con - 3) / 3   ; *Assign division quotient.*

5. Set a breakpoint at the first **MOV** instruction, then run the code and repeatedly click the **Step Into** button twice – to execute two consecutive instructions at a time

6. Examine the Registers and Watch windows to see values moved into the two CPU registers

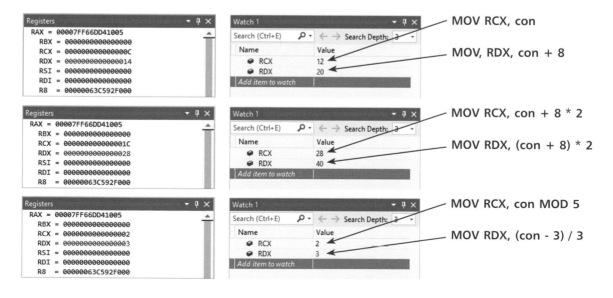

MOV RCX, con

MOV, RDX, con + 8

MOV RCX, con + 8 * 2

MOV RDX, (con + 8) * 2

MOV RCX, con MOD 5

MOV RDX, (con - 3) / 3

Exchanging Data

The Assembly **XCHG** instruction can be used to exchange data between a register and a memory variable, or between two registers. The **XCHG** instruction requires two operands, and has this syntax:

> **XCHG**   *Destination , Source*

- **Destination** – a register name if the source is a memory variable or another register, or a memory variable if the source is a register.

- **Source** – a register name if the destination is a memory variable or another register, or a memory variable if the destination is a register.

It is important to recognize that both operands must be of the same size. Assigning a variable to a 64-bit register therefore requires the variable to be 64 bits in size.

Additionally, note that the **XCHG** instruction cannot be used to exchange data between two memory variables, and you cannot use an immediate value as an operand to the **XCHG** instruction.

Improving Performance

Although the previous examples in this chapter have demonstrated the use of variables and constants in Assembly programming, you should remember that variables use system memory – which is slower to access than registers. It is, therefore, more efficient to use registers for data storage whenever possible.

The previous examples in this chapter have also used entire 64-bit registers to store data, even though simple data values do not require such large capacity. It is more economical to use fractions of a 64-bit register whenever possible – for example, using the 8-bit low-byte and 8-bit high-byte fractions of a single register, rather than using two 64-bit registers.

In Assembly programming, the adage "less is more" was never more true. Always consider using the minimum of resources for maximum efficiency and economy.

All registers are listed in the table on page 12.

1 Launch Visual Studio, then select **Create a new project** and choose the **MASM Template** you created previously

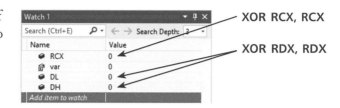

ASM
XCHG

2 Name the project "XCHG" (without the quote marks), then open the **Source.asm** file in the editor window

3 In the .**DATA** section of the file, add this line to create an uninitialized variable – by default a zero value
var QWORD ?

XOR RCX, RCX

XOR RDX, RDX

4 In the .**CODE main** procedure, insert instructions to clear two registers then assign and exchange values
XOR RCX, RCX
XOR RDX, RDX
MOV RCX, 5
XCHG RCX, var
MOV DL, 3
XCHG DH, DL

MOV RCX, 5

XCHG RCX, var

5 Set a breakpoint at the first **MOV** instruction, then run the code and click the **Step Into** button

MOV DL, 3

6 Examine the Watch window to see values moved and exchanged in the registers

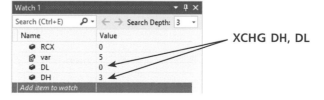

XCHG DH, DL

39

Summary

- Assembly 64-bit programming for Windows requires the Microsoft Macro Assembler (MASM) and Microsoft Linker.

- The Visual Studio IDE includes the Microsoft Macro Assembler file **ml64.exe** and Microsoft Linker file **link.exe**.

- A Visual Studio project template can be created for Assembly programming in a source code file named **Source.asm**.

- An Assembly source code file can begin with an **INCLUDELIB** directive to nominate a library file to be imported.

- The **.DATA** section of the Assembly source code file can contain variable declarations and further directives.

- The **.CODE** section of the Assembly source code file contains the Assembly language instructions to be executed.

- The **x64** toolbar option must be selected to run 64-bit Assembly programs in the Visual Studio IDE.

- The Assembly **MOV** instruction can be used to assign data to a register or to a memory variable.

- Variables must adhere to the naming convention and may be initialized upon declaration, or assigned **?** for initialization later.

- A variable declaration must specify a data allocation size, such as with the **QWORD** directive to allocate 64 bits of storage.

- Setting a breakpoint in the Visual Studio IDE allows an Assembly program to be run one line at a time.

- Registers and Watch windows can be used to display the changes made by each Assembly instruction.

- A constant is declared by specifying the **EQU** directive and a fixed value.

- Assignment expressions can include numeric operators and parentheses to specify the order of operation.

- The **XCHG** instruction can be used to exchange data between a register and a memory variable, or between two registers.

3 Performing Arithmetic

This chapter describes how to perform arithmetic on register values in Assembly language programs.

Adding & Subtracting

Addition

The Assembly **ADD** instruction can be used to add a value to a register or a memory variable. The **ADD** instruction requires two operands and has this syntax:

ADD	*Destination* , *Source*

- **Destination** – a register name if the source is a memory variable, an immediate value or another register, or a memory variable if the source is a register or an immediate value.

- **Source** – a register name or an immediate value if the destination is a memory variable or another register, or a memory variable if the destination is a register.

It is important to recognize that both operands must be of the same size. Assigning a variable to a 64-bit register therefore requires the variable to be 64 bits in size.

Additionally, note that the **ADD** instruction cannot be used to add values between two memory variables.

Subtraction

The Assembly **SUB** instruction can be used to subtract a value from a register or a memory variable. The **SUB** instruction requires two operands and has this syntax:

SUB	*Destination* , *Source*

- **Destination** – a register name if the source is a memory variable, an immediate value or another register, or a memory variable if the source is a register or an immediate value.

- **Source** – a register name or an immediate value if the destination is a memory variable or another register, or a memory variable if the destination is a register.

Both operands must be of the same size, and the **SUB** instruction cannot be used to subtract values between two memory variables.

Hot tip

If you accidentally attempt to use operands of different sizes, Visual Studio will not run the code, and its Error List window will tell you "instruction operands must be the same size".

...cont'd

ASM

ADDSUB

1 Create a new project named "ADDSUB" from the **MASM Template**, then open the **Source.asm** file

2 In the **.DATA** section of the file, add the following line to create an initialized variable
var QWORD 64

3 In the **.CODE main** procedure, insert instructions to clear two registers then add and subtract values
XOR RCX, RCX
XOR RDX, RDX
MOV RCX, 36
ADD RCX, var
MOV RDX, 400
ADD RDX, RCX
SUB RCX, 100

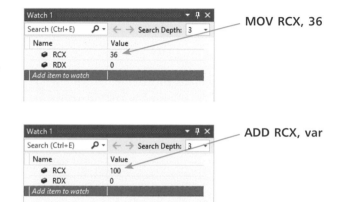

MOV RCX, 36

ADD RCX, var

4 Set a breakpoint at the first **MOV** instruction, then run the code and click the **Step Into** button

MOV RDX, 400

5 Examine the Watch window to see values added and subtracted in the registers

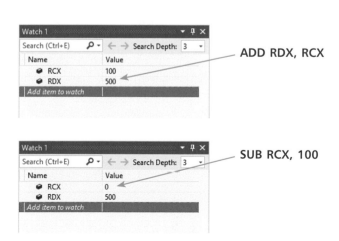

ADD RDX, RCX

SUB RCX, 100

43

Incrementing & Negating

Increment

The Assembly **INC** instruction can be used to add 1 to the value in a register or a memory variable. The **INC** instruction requires only one operand and has this syntax:

INC *Destination*

- **Destination** – a register name, or a memory variable.

Note that the **INC** instruction cannot be used to increment an immediate value.

Decrement

The Assembly **DEC** instruction can be used to subtract 1 from the value in a register or a memory variable. The **DEC** instruction requires only one operand and has this syntax:

DEC *Destination*

- **Destination** – a register name, or a memory variable.

Note that the **DEC** instruction cannot be used to decrement an immediate value.

Negate

The Assembly **NEG** instruction can be used to reverse the sign of the value in a register or a memory variable. The **NEG** instruction requires only one operand and has this syntax:

NEG *Destination*

- **Destination** – a register name, or a memory variable.

Note that the **NEG** instruction cannot be used to reverse the sign of an immediate value.

With the **NEG** instruction, a positive value becomes negative, a negative value becomes positive, and zero remains zero.

You can add format specifiers to Watch window items to control how values are displayed. Suffix the item name with a **,** comma then **d** for decimal, or **x** for hexadecimal, or **b** for binary, or **bb** for binary without leading **0b** characters.

INCNEG

1 Create a new project named "INCNEG" from the **MASM Template**, then open the **Source.asm** file

2 In the **.DATA** section of the file, add the following line to create an initialized variable
var QWORD 99

3 In the **.CODE main** procedure, insert instructions to clear one register then increment, decrement and negate values
XOR RCX, RCX
INC var
MOV RCX, 51
DEC RCX
NEG RCX

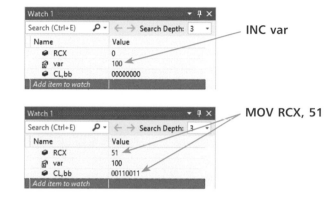

INC var

MOV RCX, 51

4 Set a breakpoint at the **INC** instruction, then run the code and click the **Step Into** button

DEC RCX

5 Examine the Watch window to see values incremented, decremented and negated

NEG RCX

6 Drag and drop the final binary value of the lower 8-bit part of the **RCX** register (**CL**) in the Watch window to see a new watch item displaying the negated decimal value

Multiplying & Dividing

Multiplication

The Assembly **MUL** instruction can be used to multiply an unsigned value in a register or a memory variable. The **MUL** instruction requires just one operand and has this syntax:

MUL *Multiplier*

- **Multiplier** – a register name or a memory variable containing the number by which to multiply a multiplicand.

The multiplicand (number to be multiplied) should be placed in a specific register matching the multiplier's size. The multiplication process places the upper half and lower half of the result in two specific registers – the result is twice the size of the multiplicand.

Multiplier	Multiplicand	=Upper Half	=Lower Half
8-bit	AL	AH	AL
16-bit	AX	DX	AX
32-bit	EAX	EDX	EAX
64-bit	RAX	RDX	RAX

Division

The Assembly **DIV** instruction can be used to divide an unsigned value in a register or a memory variable. The **DIV** instruction requires just one operand and has this syntax:

DIV *Divisor*

- **Divisor** – a register name or a memory variable containing the number by which to divide a dividend.

The dividend (the number to be divided) should be placed in a specific register matching the divisor's size, as with the multiplicand in the table above. The division process places the resulting quotient in the lower half register **AL**, **AX**, **EAX**, or **RAX** and any remainder in the associated upper half register **AH**, **DX**, **EDX** or **RDX**.

The **MUL** and **DIV** instructions perform operations on unsigned numbers. For multiplication of signed numbers you must use the **IMUL** instruction described on page 48, and for division of signed numbers you must use the **IDIV** instruction described on page 50.

1 Create a new project named "MULDIV" from the **MASM Template**, then open the **Source.asm** file

ASM
MULDIV

2 In the **.DATA** section of the file, add the following line to create an initialized variable
var QWORD 2

3 In the **.CODE main** procedure, insert instructions to clear one register then multiply and divide values
XOR RDX, RDX
MOV RAX, 10
MOV RBX, 5
MUL RBX
MUL var
MOV RBX, 8
DIV RBX

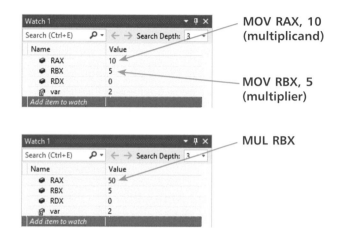

MOV RAX, 10 (multiplicand)

MOV RBX, 5 (multiplier)

MUL RBX

4 Set a breakpoint at the first **MUL** instruction, then run the code and click the **Step Into** button

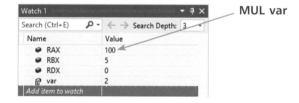

MUL var

5 Examine the Watch window to see values multiplied and divided

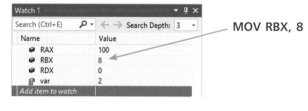

MOV RBX, 8

6 See any remainder following a division get placed in the **RDX** register

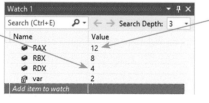

DIV RBX (quotient)

47

Multiplying Signed Numbers

The Assembly **IMUL** instruction can be used to multiply a signed value in a register or a memory variable. The **IMUL** instruction can accept one operand, with this syntax:

IMUL	*Multiplier*

- **Multiplier** – a register name, a memory variable, or an immediate value specifying the number by which to multiply the multiplicand.

With one operand, the multiplicand (the number to be multiplied) should be placed in a specific register matching the multiplier's size, following the same pattern as that for the **MUL** instruction described in the previous example on pages 46-47.

The **IMUL** instruction can accept two operands, with this syntax:

IMUL	*Multiplicand* , *Multiplier*

- **Multiplicand** – a register name containing the number to be multiplied.

- **Multiplier** – a register name, a memory variable, or an immediate value specifying the number by which to multiply the multiplicand.

The **IMUL** instruction can accept three operands, with this syntax:

IMUL	*Destination* , *Multiplicand* , *Multiplier*

- **Destination** – a register name where the result will be placed.

- **Multiplicand** – a register name or memory variable containing the number to be multiplied.

- **Multiplier** – an immediate value specifying the number by which to multiply the multiplicand.

It is important to note that the multiplicand and multiplier (and destination in the three-operand format) must be the same bit size. Additionally, note that when using the two-operand format, the result may be truncated if it's too large for the multiplicand register. If this occurs, the "overflow flag" and the "carry flag" will be set, so these can be checked if you receive an unexpected result.

The overflow flag and carry flag are described and demonstrated on page 60.

...cont'd

1 Create a new project named "IMUL" from the **MASM Template**, then open the **Source.asm** file

ASM

IMUL

2 In the **.DATA** section of the file, add the following line to create an initialized variable
var QWORD 4

3 In the **.CODE main** procedure, insert instructions to clear two registers then multiply values
XOR RAX, RAX
XOR RBX, RBX
MOV RAX, 10
MOV RBX, 2
IMUL RBX
IMUL RAX, var
IMUL RAX, RBX, -3

MOV RBX, 2

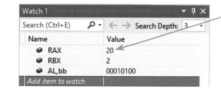

IMUL RBX

4 Set a breakpoint at the first **IMUL** instruction, then run the code and click the **Step Into** button

IMUL RBX, var

5 Examine the Watch window to see the values multiplied

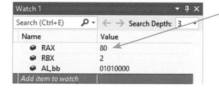

IMUL RAX, RBX, -3

6 Drag and drop the final binary value of the lower 8-bit part of the **RAX** register (**AL**) in the Watch window to see a new watch item displaying the negative decimal result

Dividing Signed Numbers

The Assembly **IDIV** instruction can be used to divide a signed value in a register or a memory variable. The **IDIV** instruction requires just one operand and has this syntax:

IDIV	*Divisor*

- **Divisor** – a register name or a memory variable specifying the number by which to divide the dividend.

The dividend (the number to be divided) should be placed in a specific register or registers twice the size of the divisor. The division process places the resulting quotient and any remainder in two specific registers.

Divisor	Dividend	=Remainder	=Quotient
8-bit	AX	AH	AL
16-bit	DX:AX	DX	AX
32-bit	EDX:EAX	EDX	EAX
64-bit	RDX:RAX	RDX	RAX

Don't forget

For multiplication or division of unsigned numbers, use the **MUL** and **DIV** instructions described on page 46.

Dividing signed numbers can produce unexpected or incorrect results, as the Most Significant Bit denoting whether the number is positive or negative may not be preserved. To avoid this, the sign bit can first be copied into the register that will contain any remainder after the division is done, to preserve the sign. You can achieve this by checking if the sign bit is **1** or **0**, then adding an appropriate instruction. For example, **MOV RDX, -1** will fill all bits in the **RDX** with 1s, denoting that the dividend in **RAX** is a negative value. This effectively extends one register into two registers – one containing the number and the other denoting that number's sign. For convenience, the Assembly language provides these sign extension instructions to implement the process:

Instruction	Converts	Extends
CBW	byte to word	AL -> AH:AL
CWD	word to double word	AX -> DX:AX
CDQ	double word to quadword	EAX -> EDX:EAX
CQO	quadword to octoword	RAX -> RDX:RAX

1 Create a new project named "IDIV" from the **MASM Template**, then open the **Source.asm** file

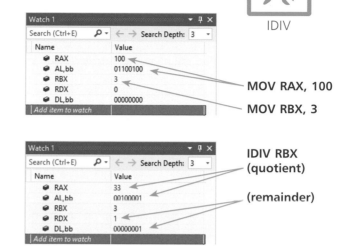

2 In the .**CODE main** procedure, insert instructions to clear three registers then divide two values
XOR RAX, RAX
XOR RBX, RBX
XOR RDX, RDX
MOV RAX, 100
MOV RBX, 3
IDIV RBX
MOV RAX, -100
CQO
IDIV RBX

MOV RAX, 100

MOV RBX, 3

IDIV RBX (quotient)

(remainder)

3 Set a breakpoint at the first **IDIV** instruction, then run the code and click the **Step Into** button

MOV RAX, -100

4 Examine the Watch window to see the values divided

CQO

5 Drag and drop the final binary value of the 8-bit parts of the **RAX** an **RDX** registers in the Watch window to see new watch items displaying the negative quotient and remainder

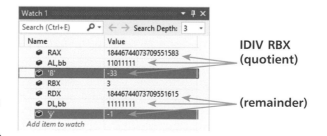

IDIV RBX (quotient)

(remainder)

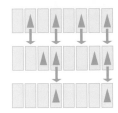

Modifying Bits

It is possible to manipulate individual bits of a binary number by performing "bitwise" operations with Assembly's logical **AND, OR, XOR** (eXclusive OR), and **NOT** instructions.

The logical instructions compare the bits in two binary number operands, then modify the bits in the first operand according to the result of the comparison.

Additionally, there is a **TEST** instruction that works the same as **AND** but does not change the value in the first operand.

The logical operations and test operation are described in detail on page 18, and the corresponding Assembly instructions are listed in the table below together with a description of each operation:

The **TEST** instruction is useful to test if a number is odd or even, without changing its value – see page 64.

Instruction	Binary Number Operation
AND	Return a **1** in each bit where <u>both</u> of two compared bits is a **1**. For example... **1010 and 1000** becomes **1000**
OR	Return a **1** in each bit where <u>either</u> of two compared bits is a **1**. For example... **1010 or 0101** becomes **1111**
XOR	Return a **1** in each bit only when the two compared bits differ, otherwise return a **0**. For example: **1110 XOR 0100** becomes **1010**
NOT	Return a **1** in each bit that is **0**, and return a **0** in each bit that is **1** – reversing the bit values. For example: **not 1010** becomes **0101**

An **AND** comparison of the numerical value in the Least Significant Bit with binary **0001b** (hexadecimal **01h**) will return **0** if the number is even, or **1** if the number is odd.

The **XOR** instruction is useful to zero an entire register by specifying the same register name for both operands – guaranteeing that no compared bits will differ, so all bits in the register will be set to zero.

1 Create a new project named "LOGIC" from the **MASM Template**, then open the **Source.asm** file

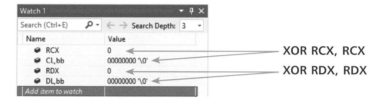

ASM

LOGIC

2 In the **.CODE main** procedure, insert instructions to manipulate bit values
XOR RCX, RCX
XOR RDX, RDX
MOV RCX, 0101b
MOV RDX, 0011b
XOR RCX, RDX
AND RCX, RDX
OR RCX, RDX

3 Set a breakpoint at the first **MOV** instruction, then run the code to see zero values initially appear in the registers

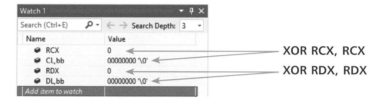

XOR RCX, RCX

XOR RDX, RDX

4 Next, click the **Step Into** button – to see two registers receive initial bit values

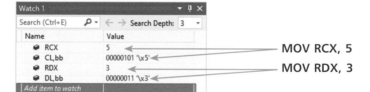

MOV RCX, 5

MOV RDX, 3

5 Click the **Step Into** button again to see the result of an **XOR** operation

XOR RCX, RDX

6 Click the **Step Into** button once more to see the result of an **AND** operation

AND RCX, RDX

7 Click the **Step Into** button one last time to see the result of an **OR** operation

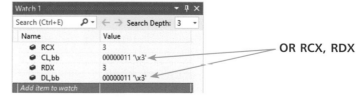

OR RCX, RDX

Shifting Bits

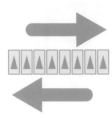

In addition to the logical operators that modify bit values, described on page 52, Assembly also provides shift instructions that move all bit values a specified number of bits in a specified direction. The **SHL** (shift left) and **SHR** (shift right) instructions accept a register and a numeric operand to specify how many bits to shift. Each shift left by one bit doubles the numerical value; each shift right by one bit halves the numerical value. For example, the instruction **SHL** *Register-Name,* **1** moves the bit values in the register one bit to the left:

128	64	32	16	8	4	2	1	Value
0	0	0	1	1	0	0	0	24 decimal

128	64	32	16	8	4	2	1	Value
0	0	1	1	0	0	0	0	48 decimal

Instruction	Binary Number Operation
SHL	Shift Left: Move each bit that is a **1** a specified number of bits to the left
SHR	Shift Right: Move each bit that is a **1** a specified number of bits to the right
SAL	Shift Arithmetic Left: Move each bit that is a **1** a specified number of bits to the left
SAR	Shift Arithmetic Right: Move each bit except the MSB sign bit a specified number of bits to the right

The bit that is shifted out is moved to the "carry flag", and the previous bit in the carry flag is thrown away.

For signed numbers, the **SAL** (shift arithmetic left) works very much like the **SHL** instruction. The **SAR** (shift arithmetic right) instruction, on the other hand, shifts each bit that is a **1**, except the MSB sign bit, a specified number of places to the right. The added bit value will be the same value as the MSB sign bit – for positive numbers, it adds **0** values, and for negative, it adds **1** values.

Hot tip

The carry flag is described and demonstrated on page 60.

ASM

SHIFT

1 Create a new project named "SHIFT" from the **MASM Template**, then open the **Source.asm** file

2 In the **.DATA** section of the file, initialize three byte-size variables with binary values

```
unum BYTE 10011001b      ; Unsigned byte.
sneg SBYTE 10011001b     ; Signed negative byte.
snum SBYTE  00110011b    ; Signed positive byte.
```

3 In the **.CODE main** procedure, insert instructions to zero three registers, then assign variable values to each one

```
XOR RCX, RCX
XOR RDX, RDX
XOR R8, R8

MOV CL, unum
MOV DL, sneg
MOV R8B, snum
```

4 Now, add instructions to move the bit values by two places in each register

```
SHR CL, 2
SAR DL, 2
SAR R8, 2
```

5 Set a breakpoint at the first **MOV** instruction, then run the code to see zero values initially appear in the registers

6 Click the **Continue** button to execute all three shift instructions

7 Examine the Watch window to see the individual bit values of all three binary numbers have been shifted

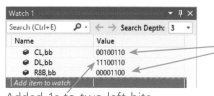

Added 0s to two left bits.

Added 1s to two left bits.

55

Rotating Bits

When shifting bits, one or more bit values are discarded as they fall off the edge and new bit values are added to the left or right – depending on the direction of shift. This is not always desirable, so x64 Assembly provides rotate instructions that move all bit values a specified number of bits in a specified direction, then move the bit values into the newly empty bits as they fall off the edge. The **ROL** (rotate left) and **ROR** (rotate right) instructions accept a register and a numeric operand to specify how many bits to rotate. For example, the instruction **ROL** *Register-Name*, **1** moves the bit values in the register one bit to the left, then places the bit value that fell off the left edge into the newly empty right-most bit:

7	6	5	4	3	2	1	0	**Bit No.**
1	0	0	1	1	0	0	0	

7	6	5	4	3	2	1	0	**Bit No.**
0	0	1	1	0	0	0	1	

Instruction	Binary Number Operation
ROL	Rotate Left: Move each bit a specified number of bits to the left, and fill them in from the right
ROR	Rotate Right: Move each bit a specified number of bits to the right, and fill them in from the left
RCL	Rotate Carry Left: Rotate left as **ROL**, but also include the carry flag in the bit rotation
RCR	Rotate Carry Right: Rotate right as **ROR**, but also include the carry flag in the bit rotation

The carry flag is described and demonstrated on page 60.

Bit rotation is useful when the program needs to retain all bit values, as it can be used to select particular bit values in a register.

1 Create a new project named "ROTATE" from the **MASM Template**, then open the **Source.asm** file

ASM

ROTATE

2 In the **.CODE main** procedure, insert an instruction to clear a single register
XOR RCX, RCX

3 Next, assign immediate values, representing ASCII character codes, to the lower and upper 8-bit fractional parts of the cleared register
MOV CL, 65
MOV CH, 90

Name	Value
CL	65 'A'
CL,bb	01000001 'A'
CH	90 'Z'
CH,bb	01011010 'Z'
CX,bb	0101101001000001

4 Now, add an instruction to rotate the 16-bit part of the register by 8 bits, effectively swapping the values in the two 8-bit fractional parts of the register
ROL CX, 8

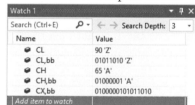

Name	Value
CL	90 'Z'
CL,bb	01011010 'Z'
CH	65 'A'
CH,bb	01000001 'A'
CX,bb	0100000101011010

5 Finally, for comparison, add instructions to rotate again, then shift the 16-bit part of the register by 8 bits
ROL CX, 8
SHR CX, 8

6 Set a breakpoint, then run the code and click the **Step Into** button

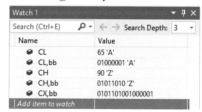

Name	Value
CL	65 'A'
CL,bb	01000001 'A'
CH	90 'Z'
CH,bb	01011010 'Z'
CX,bb	0101101001000001

7 Examine the Watch window to see the individual bits of two binary numbers rotated, then shifted off the edge

Name	Value
CL	90 'Z'
CL,bb	01011010 'Z'
CH	0 '\0'
CH,bb	00000000 '\0'
CX,bb	0000000001011010

Summary

- The **ADD** instruction requires two operands to add to a register or memory variable.

- The **SUB** instruction requires two operands to subtract from a register or memory variable.

- The **INC** instruction requires one operand to increase the value in a register or memory variable by 1.

- The **DEC** instruction requires one operand to decrease the value in a register or memory variable by 1.

- The **NEG** instruction requires one operand to reverse the sign of a value in a register or memory variable.

- The **MUL** instruction is used to multiply unsigned values and requires one operand to specify a multiplier.

- Multiplicands and dividends must be placed in a specific register that matches the size of the multiplier or divisor.

- The **DIV** instruction is used to divide unsigned values and requires one operand to specify a divisor.

- The **IMUL** instruction is used to multiply signed values and can accept one operand to specify a multiplier.

- The **IMUL** instruction can accept two operands to specify a multiplicand and a multiplier.

- The **IMUL** instruction can accept three operands to specify a destination, a multiplicand, and a multiplier.

- The **IDIV** instruction is used to divide signed values and requires one operand to specify a divisor.

- The **CBW**, **CWD**, **CDQ** and **CQO** instructions extend the registers to preserve the sign when dividing signed numbers.

- The **AND**, **OR**, **XOR** and **NOT** instructions perform logical bitwise operations on binary numbers.

- The **SHL** and **SHR** instructions shift bit values by a specified number of places.

- The **ROL** and **ROR** instructions rotate bit values by a specified number of places.

4 Directing Flow

This chapter demonstrates how Assembly instructions can examine certain conditions to determine the direction in which a program should proceed.

Observing Flags

Almost all CPUs have a "processor state" register that contains information describing the current state of the processor. In the x86-64 architecture this is a 64-bit register called **RFLAGS**. Each bit in this register is a single flag that contains a value describing if the flag is set (**1**) or not set (**0**). Many of the flags are used only by the system, but there are several useful status flags that provide information regarding previously executed instructions. To see the status flags in Visual Studio, right-click on the Registers window and select the **Flags** item on the context menu that appears.

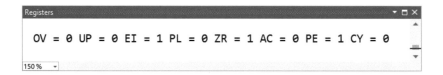

Flag	Flag Name	=1 Indicates	=0 Indicates
AC	Adjust	Auxiliary Carry	No Auxiliary Carry
CY	Carry	Carry	No Carry
EI	Enable Interrupt	Enabled	Disabled
OV	Overflow	Overflow	No Overflow
PE	Parity Even	Even	Odd
PL	Sign (polarity)	Negative	Positive
UP	Direction	Down	Up
ZR	Zero	Is Zero	Is Not Zero

There are four important status flags in Assembly programming that get set by arithmetical, logical, and comparison instructions:

- **Carry Flag** – This gets set if the result of the previous unsigned arithmetic was too large to fit within the register.

- **Overflow Flag** – This gets set if the result of the previous signed arithmetic changes the sign bit.

- **Sign Flag** – This gets set if the result of the previous instruction was a negative value.

- **Zero Flag** – This gets set if the previous result was zero.

It is essential to observe these flags, as they can pinpoint errors and inform you whether an instruction performed as expected.

Hot tip

The overflow flag is set when the MSB (sign bit) gets changed by adding two numbers with the same sign, or by subtracting two numbers with opposite signs.

...cont'd

1 Create a new project named "FLAGS" from the **MASM Template**, then open the **Source.asm** file

FLAGS

2 In the **.CODE main** procedure, insert instructions to clear a register then add and subtract values in an 8-bit register

```
XOR RCX, RCX
MOV CL, 255    ; Maximum unsigned register limit.
ADD CL, 1      ; Exceed unsigned register limit.
DEC CL         ; Return to unsigned maximum.
MOV CL, 127    ; Assign positive signed register limit.
ADD CL, 1      ; Assume negative signed register limit.
```

3 Set a breakpoint at the first **MOV** instruction, then run the code and click the **Step Into** button

4 Examine the Watch and Registers windows to see how the flags change

Watch 1	Registers	Notes
CL = 255, CL,bb = 11111111	OV = 0 UP = 0 EI = 1 PL = 0 ZR = 1 AC = 0 PE = 1 CY = 0	Default state.
CL = 0, CL,bb = 00000000	OV = 0 UP = 0 EI = 1 PL = 0 ZR = 1 AC = 1 PE = 1 **CY = 1**	Carry flag set.
CL = 255, CL,bb = 11111111	OV = 0 UP = 0 EI = 1 **PL = 1** **ZR = 0** AC = 1 PE = 1 CY = 1	Sign flag set. Zero flag cleared.
CL = 127, CL,bb = 01111111	OV = 0 UP = 0 EI = 1 PL = 1 ZR = 0 AC = 1 PE = 1 CY = 1	No change.
CL = 128, CL,bb = 10000000	**OV = 1** UP = 0 EI = 1 PL = 1 ZR = 0 AC = 1 PE = 0 CY = 0	Overflow flag set.

Making Unconditional Jumps

The CPU will, by default, execute the instructions within an Assembly program sequentially, from top to bottom. All previous examples in this book have executed in this way. As the program proceeds, the memory address of the next instruction to be executed gets stored inside a register called **RIP** (the Instruction Pointer register). After an instruction has been fetched for execution, the **RIP** register is automatically updated to point to the next instruction. You can see this register in Visual Studio's Registers window, alongside the general-purpose registers.

```
Registers                                                                          ▼ □ ×
RAX = 00007FF64B351005 RBX = 0000000000000000 RCX = 0000005F89232000 RDX = 00007FF64B351005  ▲
  RSI = 0000000000000000 RDI = 0000000000000000 R8  = 0000005F89232000 R9  = 00007FF64B351005
  R10 = 0000000000000000 R11 = 0000000000000000 R12 = 0000000000000000 R13 = 0000000000000000
  R14 = 0000000000000000 R15 = 0000000000000000 RIP = 00007FF64B351010 RSP = 0000005F8916FE88
  RBP = 0000000000000000 EFL = 00000244

  OV = 0 UP = 0 EI = 1 PL = 0 ZR = 1 AC = 0 PE = 1 CY = 0                                    ▼
100 %  ▼
```

The Assembly language provides a **JMP** (jump) instruction that can disrupt the program flow from its normal sequence by changing the memory address stored in the **RIP** register. The **JMP** instruction requires only one operand and has this syntax:

JMP	*Destination*

● **Destination** – a label, or memory address stored in a register or memory variable.

Note that the memory address is 64-bit so can only be stored in a 64-bit register or a quad word memory variable.

To specify a label as the operand to the **JMP** instruction, first add a label name of your choice, followed by a : colon character, at a point in the program at which you want to resume the flow. Then, specify that label name (without a colon) as the operand to a **JMP** instruction at the point at which you want to disrupt flow.

Where the label appears further down the program than the **JMP** instruction, any instructions between the **JMP** instruction and the label will not be executed.

This type of instruction will always jump to the destination regardless of other conditions, so they perform "unconditional branching".

Try to give labels a meaningful name, rather than "L1", "L2", etc.

...cont'd

1 Create a new project named "JMP" from the **MASM Template**, then open the **Source.asm** file

ASM

JMP

2 In the **.CODE main** procedure, insert instructions to clear two registers and to jump over two assignments
```
XOR R14, R14
XOR R15, R15
JMP next
MOV R14, 100
next:
MOV R15, final
JMP R15
MOV R14, 100
final:
```

Hot tip

The **R14** and **R15** registers are only used here because they are conveniently listed for screenshots next to the **RIP** register in the Registers window.

3 Set a breakpoint at the first **JMP** instruction, then run the code and click the **Step Into** button

4 Examine the Registers window to see memory addresses change but see that no immediate values get assigned

5 While running the code, click **Debug**, **Windows**, **Disassembly** – to open a "Disassembly" window

63

6 Select **Viewing Options** to show code, names, and addresses – to see the memory address of each instruction

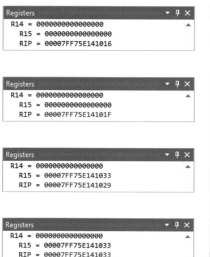

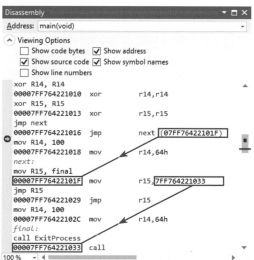

Testing Bit Values

It is possible to test individual bits of a binary number using the Assembly **TEST** instruction. This works the same as the **AND** instruction, but does not change the value in the first operand. The syntax of the **TEST** instruction looks like this:

TEST	*Destination , Source*

- **Destination** – a register or memory variable containing the binary value to be tested.

- **Source** – a register, memory variable, or immediate value containing a binary pattern for comparison.

Where the same bit in both the destination and source binary values is set to **1**, the **TEST** instruction will return a **1** – otherwise the **TEST** instruction will return **0**.

When the **TEST** instruction returns a **0**, the zero flag gets set to **1** – otherwise the zero flag gets set to **0**. For example, to test the least significant bit to determine whether the tested value is an odd number or an even number:

The status of the zero flag can be used to perform conditional branching in a program – see page 66.

Operand1:	**0111**	(decimal 7)
Operand2:	**0001**	
Test returns:	**0001**	**ZR = 0** (odd)

Conversely...

Operand1:	**1000**	(decimal 8)
Operand2:	**0001**	
Test returns:	**0000**	**ZR = 1** (even)

The same principle can be used to check whether any individual bit is set to **1** in the tested value. For example, to test whether the third bit is set in a particular binary value, like this:

Operand1:	**0111**	
Operand2:	**0100**	
Test returns:	**0100**	**ZR = 0** (bit is set)

Conversely...

Operand1:	**1000**	
Operand2:	**0100**	
Test returns:	**0000**	**ZR = 1** (bit is not set)

1 Create a new project named "TEST" from the **MASM Template**, then open the **Source.asm** file

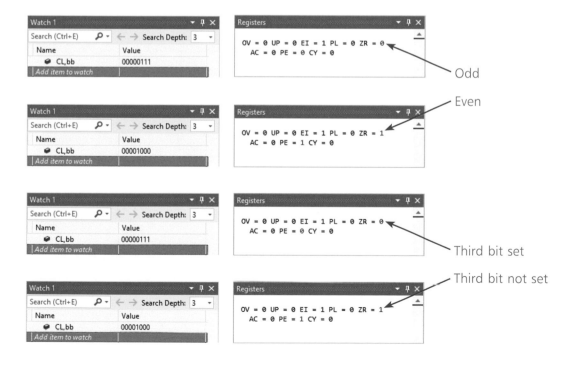

ASM

TEST

2 In the **.CODE main** procedure, insert instructions to clear one register and to test two bit values
XOR RCX, RCX
MOV RCX, 0111b
TEST RCX, 0001b
MOV RCX, 1000b
TEST RCX, 0001b
MOV RCX, 0111b
TEST RCX, 0100b
MOV RCX, 1000b
TEST RCX, 0100b

3 Set a breakpoint at the first **MOV** instruction, then run the code and repeatedly click the **Step Into** button twice – to execute two consecutive instructions at a time

4 Examine the Watch window and Registers window to see the result of each test

65

Watch 1   ▼ � ×
Search (Ctrl+E)   🔎 ▾   ← → Search Depth: 3 ▾
Name	Value
● CL,bb	00000111
Add item to watch	

Registers   ▼ ₄ ×
OV = 0 UP = 0 EI = 1 PL = 0 ZR = 0
AC = 0 PE = 0 CY = 0

Odd

Even

Watch 1   ▼ ₄ ×
Search (Ctrl+E)   🔎 ▾   ← → Search Depth: 3 ▾
Name	Value
● CL,bb	00001000
Add item to watch	

Registers   ▼ ₄ ×
OV = 0 UP = 0 EI = 1 PL = 0 ZR = 1
AC = 0 PE = 1 CY = 0

Watch 1   ▼ ₄ ×
Search (Ctrl+E)   🔎 ▾   ← → Search Depth: 3 ▾
Name	Value
● CL,bb	00000111
Add item to watch	

Registers   ▼ ₄ ×
OV = 0 UP = 0 EI = 1 PL = 0 ZR = 0
AC = 0 PE = 0 CY = 0

Third bit set

Third bit not set

Watch 1   ▼ ₄ ×
Search (Ctrl+E)   🔎 ▾   ← → Search Depth: 3 ▾
Name	Value
● CL,bb	00001000
Add item to watch	

Registers   ▼ ₄ ×
OV = 0 UP = 0 EI = 1 PL = 0 ZR = 1
AC = 0 PE = 1 CY = 0

Making Conditional Jumps

Assembly language provides several instructions that examine the condition of a flag and will jump to a nominated label or memory address only when the flag has been set – otherwise the program will proceed sequentially as normal. These types of instructions will only jump to the destination when a condition is met, so they perform "conditional branching".

Each of the instructions listed below require only one operand specifying the destination to jump to if the condition is met:

Instruction	Condition	State
JZ	Jump if zero flag is set	ZR = 1
JNZ	Jump if zero flag is NOT set	ZR = 0
JC	Jump if carry flag is set	CY = 1
JNC	Jump if carry flag is NOT set	CY = 0
JO	Jump if overflow flag is set	OV = 1
JNO	Jump if overflow flag is NOT set	OV = 0
JS	Jump if sign flag is set	PL = 1
JNS	Jump if zero flag is NOT set	PL = 0

ASM

JCOND

1 Create a new project named "JCOND" from the **MASM Template**, then open the **Source.asm** file

2 In the **.CODE main** procedure, begin by inserting instructions to clear one register, then set the carry flag and make a jump to a label
```
XOR RDX, RDX
MOV CL, 255
ADD CL, 1
JC carry
MOV RDX, 1
carry:
```

3 Next, add instructions to set the overflow flag and unset the zero flag, then jump to a label
```
MOV CL, -128
SUB CL, 1
JO overflow
MOV RDX, 2
overflow:
```

4 Now, add instructions to set the sign flag, then make two
successive jumps to labels

```
MOV CL, 255
AND CL, 10000000b
JS sign
MOV RDX, 3
sign:

JNZ notZero
MOV RDX, 4
notZero:
```

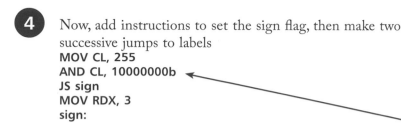

Remember to add a **b**
suffix to denote a binary
number, representing
128 decimal.

5 Set a breakpoint at the first **MOV** instruction, then run the
code and click the **Step Into** button

6 Examine the Watch window and Registers
window to see the flags get set and to see
conditional branching

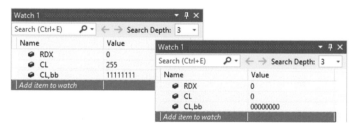

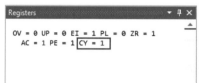

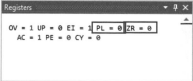

Comparing Values

The Assembly language provides a **CMP** instruction that can be used to compare two signed or unsigned numbers by performing a subtraction. It changes a combination of the flags according to the result. The syntax of the **CMP** instruction looks like this:

CMP	*Left-Operand* , *Right-Operand*

● **Left-Operand** – a register or a memory variable containing a value to be compared.

● **Right-Operand** – a register, a memory variable, or an immediate value for comparison.

After making a comparison, any of the following instructions can be issued to perform a conditional branching jump:

Instruction	Condition
JE	Jump if Left-Operand is equal to Right-Operand
JNE	Jump if Left-Operand is not equal
JA	Jump if Left-Operand is above Right-Operand
JNBE	(same as) Jump if not below or equal
JAE	Jump if Left-Operand is above or equal
JNB	(same as) Jump if not below Right-Operand
JB	Jump if Left-Operand is below Right-Operand
JNAE	(same as) Jump if not above or equal
JBE	Jump if Left-Operand is below or equal
JNA	(same as) Jump if not above Right-Operand

The simplified choice of these instructions is **JA** (jump if above), **JE** (jump if equal), and **JB** (jump if below).

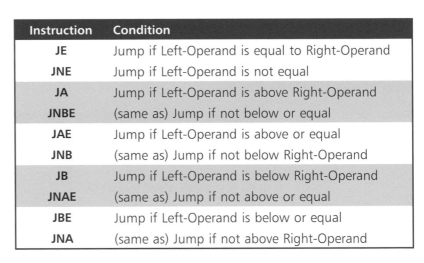

CMP

1 Create a new project named "CMP" from the **MASM Template**, then open the **Source.asm** file

2 In the **.CODE main** procedure, begin by inserting instructions to clear one register, then compare two values and make a jump to a label
```
XOR RDX, RDX
MOV RBX, 100
MOV RCX, 200
CMP RCX, RBX
JA above
MOV RDX, 1
above:
```

3 Next, add instructions to again compare two values and make a jump to a label

MOV RCX, 50
CMP RCX, RBX
JB below
MOV RDX, 2
below:

4 Now, add instructions to compare two values once more, and make a jump to a label

MOV RCX, 100
CMP RCX, RBX
JBE equal
MOV RDX, 3
equal:

5 Set a breakpoint at the first **CMP** instruction, then run the code and click the **Step Into** button

6 Examine the Watch window and Registers window to see the flags get set and to see conditional branching

Comparing Signed Values

The Assembly language **CMP** instruction, introduced in the previous example that compared unsigned values, can also be used to compare signed values. The comparison can then be followed by any of the instructions below to perform conditional branching.

Instruction	Condition
JG	Jump if Left-Operand is greater
JNLE	(same as) Jump if not less or equal
JGE	Jump if Left-Operand is greater or equal
JNL	(same as) Jump if not less than Right-Operand
JL	Jump if Left-Operand is less than Right-Operand
JNGE	(same as) Jump if not greater or equal
JLE	Jump if Left-Operand is less or equal
JNG	(same as) Jump if not greater

ASM

JSIGN

1 Create a new project named "JSIGN" from the **MASM Template**, then open the **Source.asm** file

2 In the **.CODE main** procedure, begin by inserting instructions to clear one register, then compare two values and make a jump to a label
```
XOR RDX, RDX
MOV RBX, -4
MOV RCX, -1
CMP RCX, RBX
JG greater
MOV RDX, 1
greater:
```

3 Next, add instructions to again compare two values and make a jump to a label
```
MOV RCX, -16
CMP RCX, RBX
JL less
MOV RDX, 2
less:
```

4 Now, add instructions to compare two values once more, and make a jump to a label

```
MOV RCX, -4
CMP RCX, RBX
JLE equal
MOV RDX, 3
equal:
```

5 Finally, add instructions to compare the same two values but not make a jump to a label – as the comparison fails

```
CMP RCX, RBX
JNLE notLessOrEqual
MOV RDX, 4
notLessOrEqual:
```

Hot tip

In many situations, the **JMP**, **JE**, **JZ** or **JNE** jump instructions may be sufficient.

6 Set a breakpoint at the first **CMP** instruction, then run the code and click the **Step Into** button

7 Examine the Watch window and Registers window to see the flags get set and to see conditional branching

Looping Structures

Placing a jump destination label earlier in an Assembly program than a jump instruction will cause the program to loop – repeatedly executing all instructions between the jump destination label and the jump instruction (the "loop body"). It is essential that the loop body contains a way to exit the loop to avoid creating an infinite loop that will loop forever. This can be achieved by including a jump instruction within the loop body whose destination label is located after the loop. For example:

```
MOV RCX, 1      ; counter
start:          ; loop label
loop body
INC RCX         ; increment count
CMP RCX, 10     ; compare to maximum
JE finish       ; exit if maximum
JMP start       ; or loop again
finish:         ; exit label
```

If the loop simply decrements a counter until it reaches zero, a **JNZ** instruction can be used to both loop and exit, like this:

```
MOV RCX, 10     ; counter
start:          ; loop label
loop body
DEC RCX         ; decrement count
JNZ start       ; loop again or exit
```

The Assembly language actually provides a **LOOP** instruction that has this syntax:

> **LOOP**   *Destination*

The **loop** instruction expects that the **RCX** register will always contain the loop counter. Each time a **LOOP** instruction is executed, the counter value in the **RCX** register is automatically decremented. When the counter value reaches zero, the loop will then exit. This means that the loop example above can also be created like this:

```
MOV RCX, 10
start:
loop body
LOOP start
```

The **LOOP** instruction is restrictive, however, as its loop must always end when the counter reaches zero, not any other number.

Beware

With all loop structures there must be an instruction within the loop body that will cause the loop to end.

72

1 Create a new project named "LOOP" from the **MASM Template**, then open the **Source.asm** file

LOOP

2 In the **.CODE main** procedure, insert instructions to clear a register then loop three times – copying the counter value in the loop body on each iteration of the loop

```
XOR RDX, RDX
MOV RCX, 0
start:
MOV RDX, RCX
INC RCX
CMP RCX, 3
JE finish
JMP start
finish:
```

3 Set a breakpoint at the first **MOV** instruction, then run the code and repeatedly click the **Step Into** button

4 Examine the Watch window to see the counter value copied on each iteration – until the counter reaches three and the loop ends

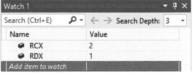

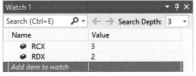

Summary

- The **RFLAGS** register contains information describing the current state of the CPU in bits that are set (**1**) or unset (**0**).

- The Carry, Overflow, Sign, and Zero flags are useful as they get set by arithmetical, logical, and comparison instructions.

- The **RIP** register contains the memory address of the next instruction to be executed.

- The **JMP** instruction requires one operand to specify a label name or memory address at which to continue execution.

- The label name at the point at which to resume flow must have a : colon suffix.

- The **JMP** instruction will always disrupt sequential program flow to perform unconditional branching.

- The **TEST** instruction requires two operands to compare the bits of a binary value against a binary pattern.

- The **TEST** instruction returns **1** if the same bit in both operands is **1**, otherwise the **TEST** instruction returns **0**.

- The **CMP** instruction compares two signed or unsigned numbers by performing subtraction.

- The **CMP** instruction can be followed by a jump instruction (such as **JE**, **JNE** or **JZ**) to disrupt sequential program flow.

- A jump instruction will only disrupt sequential program flow when a condition is met – to perform conditional branching.

- Jump instructions (such as **JG** or **JL**) can perform conditional branching following comparison of signed numbers.

- A jump destination label can be placed earlier in an Assembly program than its jump instruction – to create a loop structure.

- The **JNZ** instruction can be used to decrement a loop counter to zero, then exit the loop to resume normal program flow.

- The **LOOP** instruction decrements a loop counter in the **RCX** register and will exit when the counter reaches zcro.

5 Addressing Options

This chapter describes various ways in which to address data in Assembly language programs.

Addressing Modes

For Assembly instructions that require two operands, typically the first operand is the destination (either a register or memory location) and the second operand is the source of data to process. There are several different ways to address the data to be delivered and these are known as "addressing modes":

● **Register Addressing** – specifies the name of a register containing the operand data.

● **Immediate Addressing** – specifies an immediate numeric value that is the operand data.

● **Direct Memory Addressing** – specifies a memory location containing the operand data.

● **Direct Offset Addressing** – specifies an arithmetically modified memory location containing the operand data.

● **Indirect Memory Addressing** – specifies a register that has a copy of a memory location containing the operand data.

Register, immediate, and direct addressing modes have been widely used in previous examples to specify register names, immediate numeric values, and variable names as operands.

Direct offset addressing mode uses arithmetic operators in the instruction to modify a memory location. For example, `var+3` references the memory address three places above the address of the `var` variable.

The Assembly **LEA** (Load Effective Address) instruction can be used to retrieve the memory address of a variable. The **LEA** instruction can accept two operands, with this syntax:

LEA	*Destination* **,** *Variable*

● **Destination** – the name of a register in which to store the retrieved memory address.

● **Variable** – the name of a variable containing data.

With the memory address retrieved by **LEA** stored in a register, that memory location can be used in indirect memory addressing. The register name must simply be enclosed within **[ ]** square brackets to reference the data stored at that memory location.

Hot tip

Assembly uses [ ] square bracket operators to reference data stored at a given memory address.

76

1 Create a new project named "ADDRESS" from the **MASM Template**, then open the **Source.asm** file

ADDRESS

2 In the **.DATA** section of the file, declare and initialize four one-byte size variables
a BYTE 10
b BYTE 20
c BYTE 30
d BYTE 40

3 In the **.CODE main** procedure, add instructions to zero a register then assign data to registers using direct memory addressing and direct offset addressing
XOR RDX, RDX
MOV AL, a
MOV AH, a + 3

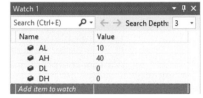

The additions are incrementing the memory locations, not adding to stored values.

4 Now, add an instruction to retrieve the memory address of the second variable and assign it to a register
LEA RCX, b

5 Finally, add instructions to assign data to registers using indirect memory addressing
MOV DL, [RCX]
MOV DH, [RCX + 1]

6 Set a breakpoint just after the final instruction of each of the three previous steps

7 Now, run the code and click the ▶ Continue ▾ **Continue** button on the Visual Studio toolbar

8 Examine the Watch and Registers windows to see values referenced by their memory address and by their offset

Addressing by Offset

Unlike a regular variable, which stores a single item of data at a single memory address, an array is a variable that stores multiple items of data at sequential memory addresses. Each item of data in an array is of the same data type specified in the array variable declaration. The declaration initializes the array by specifying the data values as a comma-separated list. For example, the following declaration initializes an array called "arr" with eight one-byte size items of data:

arr BYTE 1, 2, 4, 8, 16, 32, 64, 128

The array items are stored individually in sequential memory addresses where each address is a single byte in size:

Address	MSB 7	6	5	4	3	2	1	LSB 0	Hex
00000050	0	0	0	0	0	0	0	1	01h
00000051	0	0	0	0	0	0	1	0	02h
00000052	0	0	0	0	0	1	0	0	04h
00000053	0	0	0	0	1	0	0	0	08h
00000054	0	0	0	1	0	0	0	0	10h
00000055	0	0	1	0	0	0	0	0	20h
00000056	0	1	0	0	0	0	0	0	40h
00000057	1	0	0	0	0	0	0	0	80h

Each item of an array is referred to as an array "element". The first element in the array above is the value 1, stored at the beginning of the memory – at the first memory address.

The array name references only the first element of an array, which in this case means that **arr** references the value 1. Other elements can be referenced by adding an offset value to the array name. For example, here **arr+3** references the value 8.

The offset is simply incremented to reference each element in turn when the array is of the **BYTE** data type. For other data types, the offset must also be multiplied by the number of bytes each element comprises. For example, each element of an array of the **WORD** data type has two bytes, so the offset must be incremented and also multiplied by two to reference each element in turn.

Hot tip

Multiply the offset by four for the **DWORD** data type, and multiply the offset by eight for the **QWORD** data type.

1 Create a new project named "ARR" from the **MASM Template**, then open the **Source.asm** file

ASM

ARR

2 In the **.DATA** section of the file, declare and initialize four array variables
arrA BYTE 1, 2, 3
arrB WORD 10, 20, 30
arrC DWORD 100, 200, 300
arrD QWORD 1000, 2000, 3000

3 In the **.CODE main** procedure, add instructions to assign the first element of each array to registers
MOV CL, arrA
MOV DX, arrB
MOV R8D, arrC
MOV R9, arrD

4 Next, add instructions to assign the second element of each array to registers
MOV CL, arrA + 1
MOV DX, arrB + 2
MOV R8D, arrC + 4
MOV R9, arrD + 8

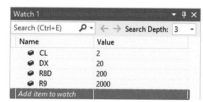

5 Finally, add instructions to assign the third element of each array to registers
MOV CL, arrA + (2 * 1)
MOV DX, arrB + (2 * 2)
MOV R8D, arrC + (2 * 4)
MOV R9, arrD +(2 * 8)

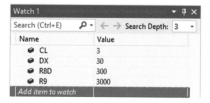

6 Set a breakpoint just after the final **MOV** instruction of each of the three previous steps

7 Now, run the code and click the **Continue** button on the Visual Studio toolbar

8 Examine the Watch window to see values referenced by their memory address and by their offset

Addressing by Order

Array variables contain a linear one-dimensional collection of elements. They can, however, represent two-dimensional arrays containing rows and columns of elements – like the values within the cells of this grid:

1A	2A	3A	4A
1B	2B	3B	4B
1C	2C	3C	4C

The element values in the grid can be stored in an array variable in one of two ways:

Row-Major Order
The first row is placed at the beginning of memory, and is followed by subsequent rows:

1A	2A	3A	4A	1B	2B	3B	4B	1C	2C	3C	4C

To reference an element in row-major order, the element's row offset must be added to the column offset. For example, to reference the **2B** value in row-major order, see that it is offset by 1 from the beginning of the second row and each row has four columns. This means that **2B** is five elements from the beginning of memory in row-major order.

Column-Major Order
The first column is placed at the beginning of memory, and is followed by subsequent columns:

1A	1B	1C	2A	2B	2C	3A	3B	3C	4A	4B	4C

To reference an element in column-major order, the element's column offset must be added to the row offset. For example, to reference the **2B** value in row-major order, see that it is offset by 1 from the beginning of the second column and each column has three rows. This means that **2B** is four elements from the beginning of memory in column-major order.

Where each element is of the **BYTE** data type, any element can be referenced by adding the total offset to the array name. For other data types, the offset must also be multiplied by the number of bytes each element comprises – as with the previous example.

Multi-dimensional arrays with more than two indices can produce hard-to-read source code and may lead to errors.

1 Create a new project named "ARR2D" from the **MASM Template**, then open the **Source.asm** file

ASM

ARR2D

2 In the **.DATA** section of the file, declare and initialize four array variables with the same values, ordered differently
rows BYTE 0, 1, 2, 3,   10, 11, 12, 13,   20, 21, 22, 23
cols BYTE 0, 10, 20,   1, 11, 21,   2, 12, 22,   3, 13, 23
arrA DWORD 0, 1, 2, 3,   10, 11, 12, 13,   20, 21, 22, 23
arrB DWORD 0, 10, 20,   1, 11, 21,   2, 12, 22,   3, 13, 23

3 In the **.CODE main** procedure, add instructions to assign the first element of each array to registers
MOV CL, rows
MOV CH, cols
MOV R8D, arrA
MOV R9D, arrB

Watch 1	▾ ₽ ×
Search (Ctrl+E) 🔎 ▾ ← → Search Depth: 3 ▾	
Name	Value
● CL	0
● CH	0
● R8D	0
● R9D	0
Add item to watch	

4 Next, add instructions to assign a specific element in the first two arrays to registers
MOV CL, rows + 5
MOV CH, cols + 4

Watch 1	▾ ₽ ×
Search (Ctrl+E) 🔎 ▾ ← → Search Depth: 3 ▾	
Name	Value
● CL	11
● CH	11
● R8D	0
● R9D	0
Add item to watch	

Hot tip

Two-dimensional arrays are often used to store grid coordinates.

5 Finally, add instructions to assign a specific element in the final two arrays to registers
MOV R8D, arrA + (8 * 4)
MOV R9D, arrB + (2 * 4)

Watch 1	▾ ₽ ×
Search (Ctrl+E) 🔎 ▾ ← → Search Depth: 3 ▾	
Name	Value
● CL	11
● CH	11
● R8D	20
● R9D	20
Add item to watch	

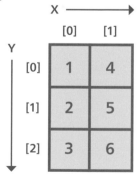

X ⟶

	[0]	[1]
Y		
[0]	1	4
[1]	2	5
[2]	3	6

6 Set a breakpoint just after the final **MOV** instruction of each of the three previous steps

7 Now, run the code and click the **Continue** button on the Visual Studio toolbar

8 Examine the Watch window to see values referenced by their memory address and by their offset

Addressing Source Index

In x64 Assembly programming, the elements in an array can be considered to have a zero-based index. So, the first value is stored in element zero, the second value is stored in element one, etc.

The value in an individual array element can be referenced by stating the array name followed by [ ] square brackets surrounding an integer specifying the index number. For example, with an array named "arr" the first element is **arr[0]**. This addresses the same memory location as the array name alone.

When the array is of the **BYTE** data type, the index number is simply incremented by 1 to reference each element in turn. For other data types, the index must also be multiplied by the number of bytes each element comprises.

Loops and arrays are perfect partners, as indirect addressing can iterate through each element in an array. There are variations of indirect addressing that use a combination of these components:

Base + Index * Scale + Displacement

- **Base** – typically, a register containing the memory address of an array.

- **Index** – a register or immediate value to specify an element index number.

- **Scale** – can specify **1** (byte), **2** (word), **4** (double word), or **8** (quad word) to match the array data type.

- **Displacement** – an immediate value can be added to denote row or column offsets in two-dimensional arrays.

The memory address of an array can best be stored in the **RSI** (Source Index) register and be used for the base component. Similarly, the **RCX** register can be used to contain a counter value for the index component. A loop can then iterate through the elements of an array by incrementing the counter on each iteration of the loop.

Usefully, Assembly provides a **LENGTHOF** operator that returns the length of a given array as a numeric value. This can be compared with the current counter value to determine when the loop has reached the final element of the array.

82

The square bracket operator [ ] returns the data stored at the memory location specified between the [and] brackets.

1 Create a new project named "INDEX" from the **MASM Template**, then open the **Source.asm** file

INDEX

2 In the **.DATA** section of the file, declare and initialize an array of quad word size elements
arr QWORD 10, 20, 30

3 In the **.CODE main** procedure, add instructions to copy the array's memory address into a register and initialize a counter register
LEA RSI, arr
MOV RCX, 0

Watch 1	▾ ♯ ✕
Search (Ctrl+E) 🔎 ▾ ← → Search Depth: 3 ▾	
Name	Value
● RSI,X	0x00007FF6BCE64000
● RCX	0
● RDX	0
Add item to watch	

4 Now, begin a loop by copying a value into a register from the address of an array element – by indirect addressing
start:
MOV RDX, [RSI + RCX * 8]

Watch 1	▾ ♯ ✕
Search (Ctrl+E) 🔎 ▾ ← → Search Depth: 3 ▾	
Name	Value
● RSI,X	0x00007FF6BCE64000
● RCX	0
● RDX	10
Add item to watch	

5 Finally, complete the loop by incrementing the counter and testing if the final element has been reached
INC RCX
CMP RCX, LENGTHOF arr
JNE start

Watch 1	▾ ♯ ✕
Search (Ctrl+E) 🔎 ▾ ← → Search Depth: 3 ▾	
Name	Value
● RSI,X	0x00007FF6BCE64000
● RCX	1
● RDX	20
Add item to watch	

6 Set a breakpoint at the **LEA** instruction

Watch 1	▾ ♯ ✕
Search (Ctrl+E) 🔎 ▾ ← → Search Depth: 3 ▾	
Name	Value
● RSI,X	0x00007FF6BCE64000
● RCX	2
● RDX	30
Add item to watch	

7 Now, run the code and click the **Step Into** button on the Visual Studio toolbar

8 Examine the Watch window to see the loop iterate through each element of the array

Addressing Destination Index

Just as indirect addressing is used in the previous example to loop through an array, it can be used to fill the elements of an array. In this case, the memory address of the array can best be stored in the **RDI** (Destination Index) register and be used for the base component. The **RCX** register can be used to contain a counter value for the index component, as in the previous example.

To declare an array in which each element contains the same initial value, Assembly provides a **DUP** (duplicate) operator. This must be preceded by the number of elements required, and followed by their initial value within **( )** parentheses. For example, the declaration **arr BYTE 10 DUP (0)** creates an array of 10 one-byte size elements that each contain a **0**.

With two arrays of the same data type, you can easily copy element values from one array to the other using the appropriate special copying instruction **MOVSB** (byte), **MOVSW** (word), **MOVSD** (double word) or **MOVSQ** (quad word). These each copy a value from a Source Index address to a Destination Index address.

Usefully, Assembly also provides a **REP** instruction that repeats the instruction supplied as its operand the number of times specified in the count register. Its syntax looks like this:

REP	*Instruction*

This can be used to move multiple array element values by specifying one of the copying instructions as the operand to the **REP** instruction.

FILL

1 Create a new project named "FILL" from the **MASM Template**, then open the **Source.asm** file

2 In the **.DATA** section of the file, declare and initialize two arrays of quad word size elements with zeros
arr QWORD 0, 0, 0
cpy QWORD 3 DUP (0)

3 In the **.CODE main** procedure, begin by copying the first array's memory address into a register, then initialize a loop counter and a data value
LEA RDI, arr
MOV RCX, 0
MOV RDX, 10

...cont'd

4 Next, add a loop that copies a value from a register into the address of an array element (using indirect addressing) and increments the value to be copied and the counter

start:
```
MOV [RDI+RCX* 8], RDX
ADD RDX, 10
INC RCX
CMP RCX, LENGTHOF arr
JNE start
```

Name	Value
R10	0
R11	0
R12	0
R13	0
R14	0
R15	0

5 Now, assign each element value to a register
```
MOV R10, arr[ 0 * 8 ]
MOV R11, arr[ 1 * 8 ]
MOV R12, arr[ 2 * 8 ]
```

Name	Value
R10	10
R11	20
R12	30
R13	0
R14	0
R15	0

6 Then, copy all the first array's filled element values into the second array elements
```
LEA RSI, arr
LEA RDI, cpy
MOV RCX, LENGTHOF arr
CLD ◄
REP MOVSQ
```

Hot tip

Issue a **CLD** (clear direction flag) instruction before copying instructions, to ensure the elements will be incremented in memory, not decremented. See page 88 for details.

7 Finally, assign each copied element value to a register
```
MOV R13, cpy[ 0 * 8 ]
MOV R14, cpy[ 1 * 8 ]
MOV R15, cpy[ 2 * 8 ]
```

Name	Value
R10	10
R11	20
R12	30
R13	10
R14	20
R15	30

8 Set breakpoints before and after each group of assignment instructions in Step 5 and Step 7

9 Now, run the code and click the **Continue** button on the Visual Studio toolbar

10 Examine the Watch window to see the loop fill each element of the first array and then copy those elements to fill the second array

Summary

- The **LEA** instruction can be used to retrieve the memory address of a variable.

- Square brackets [ ] can enclose the name of a register containing a memory address, to reference the data at that address.

- Addressing modes are different ways to address the data to be delivered.

- Register addressing specifies the name of a register containing the data to be delivered.

- Immediate addressing specifies a numeric value that is the actual data.

- Direct memory addressing specifies a memory location containing the data to be delivered.

- Direct offset addressing specifies an arithmetically modified memory location address containing the data to be delivered.

- Indirect memory addressing specifies a register that holds a memory location address containing the data to be delivered.

- An array variable can be declared as a comma-separated list of element values.

- An array variable can be declared by specifying the required number of elements and value to the **DUP** operator.

- Two-dimensional arrays can be represented in row-major order, or in column-major order.

- An array can be considered to have a zero-based index.

- An array element can be addressed by stating the array name followed by square brackets enclosing the element index number.

- Indirect addressing uses a combination of the components Base + Index * Scale + Displacement.

- The **REP** instruction repeats the instruction supplied as its operand the number of times specified in the count register.

6 Handling Strings

Moving Characters

As an ASCII text character occupies one byte of memory numerically, a text "string" of multiple characters is simply an array of bytes. The Assembly x64 programming language provides a number of instructions that enable strings of characters to be copied at a byte, word, double word, or quad word length.

The "MOVS" string copying instructions are **MOVSB** (byte), **MOVSW** (word), **MOVSD** (double word), and **MOVSQ** (quad word). These are typically combined with a **REP** instruction to repeatedly copy characters from a source to a destination.

The combined instructions are affected by the direction flag to move forward in memory if the flag is not set (**0**) or to move backward if the flag is set (**1**). A **CLD** (clear direction flag) or **STD** (set direction flag) instruction can determine the direction. It is generally preferable to move forward using the **CLD** instruction. This instruction should be issued before any combined copying instruction to ensure there will be forward movement.

To use the combined instructions, the **RSI** (source index) and **RDI** (destination index) registers must contain the starting memory address of the source and destination respectively. The **RCX** register must also contain a counter for the desired number of repetitions.

- **REP MOVSB** – repeatedly copies <u>one byte</u> from a memory location pointed to by the **RSI** register, into the memory location pointed to by the **RDI** register. It then increments (or decrements if the direction is backward) both the **RSI** and **RDI** register by <u>one</u> – until the **RCX** register becomes zero.

- **REP MOVSW** – works like **REP MOVSB** but repeatedly copies <u>one word</u>, then increments (or decrements) the **RSI** and **RDI** register by <u>two</u> – until the **RCX** register becomes zero.

- **REP MOVSD** – works like **REP MOVSB** but repeatedly copies <u>one double word</u>, then increments (or decrements) the **RSI** and **RDI** register by <u>four</u> – until the **RCX** register becomes zero.

- **REP MOVSQ** – works like **REP MOVSB** but repeatedly copies <u>one quad word</u>, then increments (or decrements) the **RSI** and **RDI** register by <u>eight</u> – until the **RCX** register becomes zero.

The **DUP** operator can create an empty array, and the **SIZEOF** operator can be used to determine the number of bytes in a string.

If a **MOVS** instruction doesn't produce the expected result, check that the direction flag is not set.

...cont'd

MOVS

1 Create a new project named "MOVS" from the **MASM Template**, then open the **Source.asm** file

2 In the **.DATA** section of the file, declare a string array and an empty array of one-byte size elements
src BYTE 'abc'
dst BYTE 3 DUP (?)

3 In the **.CODE main** procedure, add instructions to clear three registers, then set up three other registers – ready to copy characters
XOR RDX, RDX
XOR R8, R8
XOR R9, R9
LEA RSI, src
LEA RDI, dst
MOV RCX, SIZEOF src

4 Next, ensure forward movement and repeatedly copy each byte from source to destination
CLD
REP MOVSB

5 Now, assign the copied bytes to registers to confirm success of the operation
MOV DL, dst[0]
MOV R8B, dst[1]
MOV R9B, dst[2]

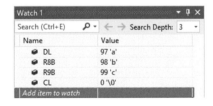

6 Set a breakpoint just after each of the three previous steps

7 Now, run the code and click the **Continue** button on the Visual Studio toolbar

8 Examine the Watch window to see the string characters have been copied into the previously empty array

Storing Contents

The Assembly x64 programming language provides a number of instructions that enable content to be stored in a memory location at a byte, word, double word, or quad word length.

The "STOS" string storing instructions are **STOSB** (byte), **STOSW** (word), **STOSD** (double word), and **STOSQ** (quad word). These are typically combined with a **REP** instruction to repeatedly store content from a source to a destination.

The combined instructions are affected by the direction flag to move forward in memory if the flag is not set (**0**) or to move backward if the flag is set (**1**). A **CLD** clear direction flag instruction should be issued before any combined storing instruction, to ensure there will be forward movement.

To use the combined instructions, the **AL, AX, EAX,** or **RAX** accumulator register must contain the value to be stored, appropriate for the size of the operation. The **RDI** register must contain the starting memory address of the destination, and the **RCX** register must contain a counter for the number of repetitions.

The **STOS** instructions are used to store data <u>into</u> memory.

- **REP STOSB** – repeatedly stores <u>one byte</u> from the **AL** register in the memory location pointed to by the **RDI** register. It then increments (or decrements if the direction is backward) the **RDI** register by <u>one</u> – until the **RCX** register becomes zero.

- **REP STOSW** – repeatedly stores <u>one word</u> from the **AX** register in the memory location pointed to by the **RDI** register. It then increments (or decrements) the **RDI** register by <u>two</u> – until the **RCX** register becomes zero.

- **REP STOSD** – repeatedly stores <u>one double word</u> from the **EAX** register in the memory location pointed to by the **RDI** register. It then increments (or decrements) the **RDI** register by <u>four</u> – until the **RCX** register becomes zero.

- **REP STOSQ** – repeatedly stores <u>one quad word</u> from the **RAX** register in the memory location pointed to by the **RDI** register. It then increments (or decrements) the **RDI** register by <u>eight</u> – until the **RCX** register becomes zero.

1 Create a new project named "STOS" from the **MASM Template**, then open the **Source.asm** file

ASM
STOS

2 In the **.DATA** section of the file, declare an empty array of one-byte size elements
dst BYTE 3 DUP (?)

3 In the **.CODE main** procedure, add instructions to clear three registers, then set up three other registers – ready to store content
XOR RDX, RDX
XOR R8, R8
XOR R9, R9
MOV AL, 'A'
LEA RDI, dst
MOV RCX, SIZEOF dst

Name	Value
DL	0 '\0'
R8B	0 '\0'
R9B	0 '\0'
CL	3 '\x3'

4 Next, ensure forward movement and repeatedly store one byte from source to destination
CLD
REP STOSB

91

5 Now, assign stored bytes to registers to confirm success of the operation
MOV DL, dst[0]
MOV R8B, dst[1]
MOV R9B, dst[2]

Name	Value
DL	65 'A'
R8B	65 'A'
R9B	65 'A'
CL	0 '\0'

6 Set a breakpoint just after each of the three previous steps

7 Now, run the code and click the **Continue** button on the Visual Studio toolbar

8 Examine the Watch window to see the content has been stored into the previously empty array

Loading Contents

The Assembly x64 programming language provides a number of instructions that enable content to be loaded from a memory location at a byte, word, double word, or quad word length.

The "LODS" string loading instructions are **LODSB** (byte), **LODSW** (word), **LODSD** (double word), and **LODSQ** (quad word). These can be combined with a **REP** instruction to repeatedly load content from a source to a destination.

The combined instructions are affected by the direction flag to move forward in memory if the flag is not set (**0**) or to move backward if the flag is set (**1**). A **CLD** clear direction flag instruction should be issued before any combined loading instruction to ensure there will be forward movement.

To use the combined instructions, the **AL**, **AX**, **EAX**, or **RAX** accumulator register is the destination in which the value will be loaded, appropriate for the size of the operation. The **RSI** register must contain the starting memory address of the source and the **RCX** register must contain a counter for the number of repetitions.

- **REP LODSB** – repeatedly loads <u>one byte</u> into the **AL** register from the memory location pointed to by the **RSI** register. It then increments (or decrements if the direction is backward) the **RSI** register by <u>one</u> – until the **RCX** register becomes zero.

- **REP LODSW** – repeatedly loads <u>one word</u> into the **AX** register from the memory location pointed to by the **RSI** register. It then increments (or decrements) the **RSI** register by <u>two</u> – until the **RCX** register becomes zero.

- **REP LODSD** – repeatedly loads <u>one double word</u> into the **EAX** register from the memory location pointed to by the **RSI** register. It then increments (or decrements) the **RSI** register by <u>four</u> – until the **RCX** register becomes zero.

- **REP LODSQ** – repeatedly loads <u>one quad word</u> into the **RAX** register from the memory location pointed to by the **RSI** register. It then increments (or decrements) the **RSI** register by <u>eight</u> – until the **RCX** register becomes zero.

As the ASCII character code values differ by 32 between lowercase and uppercase, the **LODSB** instruction can be used in a loop, along with the **STOSB** instruction to convert character case.

The **LODS** instructions are used to load data <u>from</u> memory. They are seldom useful, but exist in line with the other string instructions.

...cont'd

1 Create a new project named "LODS" from the **MASM Template**, then open the **Source.asm** file

LODS

2 In the **.DATA** section of the file, declare and initialize an array of one-byte size elements
src BYTE 'abc'

3 In the **.CODE main** procedure, add instructions to clear three registers, then set up three other registers – ready to load content
XOR RDX, RDX
XOR R8, R8
XOR R9, R9
LEA RSI, src
MOV RDI, RSI
MOV RCX, SIZEOF src

4 Next, ensure forward movement, then load each element, change it to uppercase and store it back in the array
CLD
start:
LODSB
SUB AL, 32
STOSB
DEC RCX
JNZ start

5 Now, assign stored bytes to registers to confirm success of the operation
MOV DL, src[0]
MOV R8B, src[1]
MOV R9B, src[2]

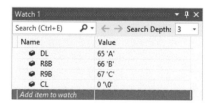

6 Set a breakpoint just after each of the three previous steps

7 Now, run the code and click the **Continue** button on the Visual Studio toolbar

8 Examine the Watch window to see the character case has been converted in each element of the array

Scanning Strings

The Assembly x64 programming language provides a number of instructions that enable content to be scanned in a memory location at a byte, word, double word, or quad word length.

The "SCAS" string scanning instructions are **SCASB** (byte), **SCASW** (word), **SCASD** (double word), and **SCASQ** (quad word). These are typically combined with a **REPNE** (repeat if not equal) instruction to repeatedly compare a source to a destination.

The combined instructions are affected by the direction flag to move forward in memory if the flag is not set (**0**) or to move backward if the flag is set (**1**). A **CLD** clear direction flag instruction should be issued before any combined scanning instruction to ensure there will be forward movement.

To use the combined instructions, the **AL**, **AX**, **EAX**, or **RAX** register should contain the value to compare against, appropriate for the size of the operation. The **RDI** register must contain the starting memory address of the source to be scanned, and the **RCX** register must contain a counter for the number of repetitions.

- **REPNE SCASB** – repeatedly compares the **AL** register against the memory location pointed to by the **RDI** register. It then increments (or decrements) the **RDI** register by <u>one</u> – until the **RCX** register becomes zero, or the value in the **AL** register matches that in the memory location.

- **REPNE SCASW** – repeatedly compares the **AX** register against the memory location pointed to by the **RDI** register. It then increments (or decrements) the **RDI** register by <u>two</u> – until the **RCX** register becomes zero, or the comparisons match.

- **REPNE SCASD** – repeatedly compares the **EAX** register against the memory location pointed to by the **RDI** register. It then increments (or decrements) the **RDI** register by <u>four</u> – until the **RCX** register becomes zero, or the comparisons match.

- **REPNE SCASQ** – repeatedly compares the **RAX** register against the memory location pointed to by the **RDI** register. It then increments (or decrements) the **RDI** register by <u>eight</u> – until the **RCX** register becomes zero, or the comparisons match.

When the scan does find a match, the zero flag gets set, and this can be used to jump to an appropriate instruction.

The position in the string of a successful match can be calculated by deducting the value at which the counter stopped from the length of the scanned string.

Hot tip

...cont'd

SCAS

1 Create a new project named "SCAS" from the **MASM Template**, then open the **Source.asm** file

2 In the **.DATA** section of the file, declare and initialize an array of one-byte size elements and an empty variable
src BYTE 'abc'
found BYTE ?

3 In the **.CODE main** procedure, add instructions to clear a register, then set up three other registers – ready to scan content
XOR RAX, RAX
MOV AL, 'b'
LEA RDI, src
MOV RCX, SIZEOF src

4 Next, ensure forward movement, then scan each element
CLD
REPNE SCASB

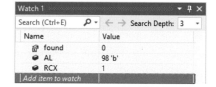

5 Now, add instructions to confirm the result of the operation
JNZ absent
MOV found, 1
JMP finish

absent:
MOV found, 0
finish:

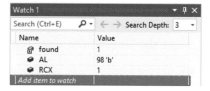

6 Set a breakpoint just after each of the three previous steps

7 Now, run the code and click the **Continue** button on the Visual Studio toolbar

8 Examine the Watch window to see a match was found – change **AL** to any letter d-z to see the comparison fail

Comparing Strings

The Assembly x64 programming language provides a number of instructions that enable strings to be compared in two memory locations at a byte, word, double word, or quad word length.

The "CMPS" string comparing instructions are **CMPSB** (byte), **CMPSW** (word), **CMPSD** (double word), and **CMPSQ** (quad word). These are typically combined with a **REPE** (repeat if equal) instruction to repeatedly compare a source to a destination.

The combined instructions are affected by the direction flag to move forward in memory if the flag is not set (**0**) or to move backward if the flag is set (**1**). A **CLD** clear direction flag instruction should be issued before any combined comparing instruction to ensure there will be forward movement.

To use the combined instructions, the **RSI** and **RDI** registers should contain the starting memory address of the strings to be compared. The **RCX** register must also contain a counter for the number of repetitions.

- **REPE CMPSB** – repeatedly compares <u>one byte</u> in the memory location pointed to by the **RSI** register against <u>one byte</u> in the memory location pointed to by the **RDI** register. It then increments (or decrements) both the **RSI** and **RDI** registers by <u>one</u> – until the **RCX** register becomes zero, or the comparison does not match.

- **REPE CMPSW** – works like **REPE CMPSB** but repeatedly compares <u>one word</u>, then increments (or decrements) the **RSI** and **RDI** register by <u>two</u> – until the **RCX** register becomes zero, or the comparison does not match.

- **REPE CMPSD** – works like **REPE CMPSB** but repeatedly compares <u>one double word</u>, then increments (or decrements) the **RSI** and **RDI** register by <u>four</u> – until the **RCX** register becomes zero, or the comparison does not match.

- **REPE CMPSQ** – works like **REPE CMPSB** but repeatedly compares <u>one quad word</u>, then increments (or decrements) the **RSI** and **RDI** register by <u>eight</u> – until the **RCX** register becomes zero, or the comparison does not match.

When the comparison does find a match, the zero flag gets set, and this can be used to jump to an appropriate instruction.

The string comparison is case-sensitive, as the ASCII character codes are numerically different for uppercase and lowercase characters.

96

1 Create a new project named "CMPS" from the **MASM Template**, then open the **Source.asm** file

CMPS

2 In the **.DATA** section of the file, declare and initialize an array of one-byte size elements and an empty variable
src BYTE 'abc'
dst BYTE 'abc'
match BYTE ?

3 In the **.CODE main** procedure, add instructions to set up three registers – ready to compare strings
LEA RSI, src
LEA RDI, dst
MOV RCX, SIZEOF src

4 Next, ensure forward movement, then compare strings
CLD
REPE CMPSB

5 Now, add instructions to confirm the result of the operation
JNZ differ
MOV match, 1
JMP finish

differ:
MOV match, 0
finish:

6 Set a breakpoint just after each of the three previous steps

7 Now, run the code and click the **Continue** button on the Visual Studio toolbar

8 Examine the Watch window to see a match was found – change any letter in a string to see the comparison fail

Summary

- A text string is an array of bytes in which each element is a byte containing a numerical ASCII character code.

- All combined string instructions that repeat are affected by the direction flag, which must be clear to move forward.

- The **CLD** instruction clears the direction flag to move forward, but the **std** instruction sets the direction flag to backward.

- The copying instructions **MOVSB**, **MOVSW**, **MOVSD**, and **MOVSQ** combined with a **REP** instruction repeatedly copy characters.

- The "MOVS" instructions use the **RSI**, **RDI**, and **RCX** registers.

- The storing instructions **STOSB**, **STOSW**, **STOSD**, and **STOSQ** combined with a **REP** instruction repeatedly store content.

- The "STOS" instructions use the **RDI** and **RCX** registers, plus **AL**, **AX**, **EAX** or **RAX** register appropriate for the size of operation.

- The loading instructions **LODSB**, **LODSW**, **LODSD**, and **LODSQ** combined with a **REP** instruction repeatedly load content.

- The "LODS" instructions use the **RSI** and **RCX** registers, plus **AL**, **AX**, **EAX** or **RAX** register appropriate for the size of operation.

- The **REPNE** instruction repeats the instruction supplied as its operand if a comparison does not match (is not equal).

- The scanning instructions **SCASB**, **SCASW**, **SCASD**, and **SCASQ** combined with a **REPNE** instruction repeatedly compare until a counter reaches zero, or until a match is found.

- The "SCAS" instructions use the **RDI** and **RCX** registers, plus **AL**, **AX**, **EAX** or **RAX** register appropriate for the size of operation.

- The **REPE** instruction repeats the instruction supplied as its operand if a comparison does match (is equal).

- The comparing instructions **CMPSB**, **CMPSW**, **CMPSD**, and **CMPSQ** combined with a **REPE** instruction repeatedly compare until a counter reaches zero, or until the comparison does not match.

- The "CMPS" instructions use the **RSI**, **RDI** and **RCX** registers.

7 Building Blocks

Stacking Items

Larger Assembly programs can usefully be broken down into smaller pieces of code called "procedures" that each perform a particular task. This makes the code easier to understand, write, and maintain. When a procedure is implemented, MASM uses the "stack" data structure to save necessary information.

Items can be added onto the top of the stack by a **PUSH** instruction, or removed from the top of the stack by a **POP** instruction. The operand to these instructions can be an immediate value, a register, or a memory location.

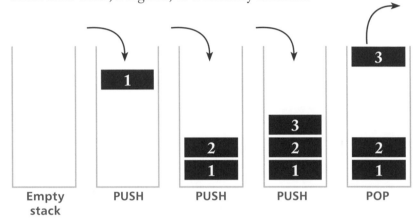

| Empty stack | PUSH | PUSH | PUSH | POP |

Items cannot be added to, or removed from, anywhere other than the top of the stack. This type of data structure is referred to as LIFO (Last In First Out) – similar to a stack of cafeteria trays.

Stack Characteristics

● Only 16-bit words or 64-bit quad words can be saved on the stack; not a double word or byte data type.

● The memory address of the top of the stack grows down to decreasing addresses (in reverse direction).

● The top of the stack points to the lower byte of the last item added to the stack.

● The **PUSH** and **POP** instructions must be used in pairs – whatever is pushed on must be popped off to avoid unbalancing the stack.

● The **RSP** register points to the top of the stack.

Don't forget

Whenever you **PUSH** an item onto the stack you must subsequently **POP** it off the stack.

...cont'd

STACK

1 Create a new project named "STACK" from the **MASM Template**, then open the **Source.asm** file

2 In the **.DATA** section of the file, initialize a variable
var WORD 256

3 In the **.CODE main** procedure, assign a value to a register, and note the empty stack memory address
MOV RAX, 64

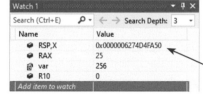

4 Next, push the assigned value onto the stack, assign a new value, then see the lower memory address of the stack top
PUSH RAX
MOV RAX, 25

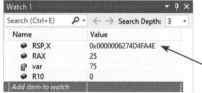

Address decreases by 8 bytes for quad word.

5 Now, push the variable value onto the stack and see the stack top memory address decrease further, then assign a new value
PUSH var
MOV var, 75

Address decreases by 2 bytes for word.

6 Finally, pop the top stack item back into the variable, then pop the new top stack item into a register – see the stack top return to its original memory address
POP var
POP R10

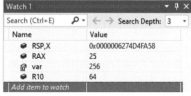

7 Set a breakpoint just after each of the four previous steps, then run the code and click the **Continue** button

8 Examine the Watch window to see values added to the stack, then removed from the stack

Calling Procedures

All previous examples in this book have placed Assembly instructions within the **main** procedure that resides in the **.CODE** section of the program. The **main** procedure is the entry point that the assembler looks for in all Assembly programs. Your own custom procedures can also be added to the **.CODE** section to make the program more flexible.

A custom procedure is given a name of your choice, following the same naming convention as that for variable names described on page 32. The name is a label that begins a procedure block declaration within the **.CODE** section of a program.

In a procedure block declaration, the procedure name is followed on the same line by a **PROC** (procedure) directive that identifies the block as being a procedure. Subsequent lines can then contain instructions to be executed by that procedure.

After the final instruction there must be a **RET** instruction telling the program to return to the point in the program from where it was called. This might be from within the main function or even another custom function.

The procedure block is terminated on a final line containing the procedure name once more, followed by an **ENDP** (end procedure) directive. The syntax of a procedure block looks like this:

Procedure-Name **PROC**
; Instructions to be executed go here.
RET
Procedure-Name **ENDP**

Values within volatile registers will not be automatically preserved after a procedure call. It is the caller's responsibility to save them elsewhere if they wish to preserve them.

A custom procedure can be called from inside any other procedure simply by stating its name after a **CALL** instruction. Interestingly, this disrupts the normal program flow by placing the address following the **CALL** instruction onto the stack, then branches to the custom procedure. After the custom procedure has executed its instructions, the **RET** instruction pops the address off the stack and passes it to the instruction pointer, which then branches to resume normal program flow at the next instruction after the **CALL** instruction.

A custom procedure can also be assigned to a 64-bit register and called by stating the register name after the **CALL** instruction.

...cont'd

1 Create a new project named "PROC" from the **MASM Template**, then open the **Source.asm** file

ASM
PROC

2 Before the **main** procedure in the .CODE section of the file, insert a custom procedure to clear the **RAX** register
```
zeroRAX PROC
XOR RAX, RAX
RET
zeroRAX ENDP
```

3 In the **main** procedure, assign a value to the **RAX** register, then call the custom procedure to clear the register
```
MOV RAX, 8
CALL zeroRAX
```

4 Set a breakpoint, run the code and click **Step Into**

5 See the stack address decrease as it stores the address of the location at which to return after the custom procedure

Watch 1	▼ ↳ ×
Search (Ctrl+E)	🔎 ← → Search Depth: 3 ▾
Name	**Value**
RSP,X	0x00000074F22FF9C8
RIP,X	0x00007FF612B4102B
RAX	8
Add item to watch	

Watch 1	▼ ↳ ×
Search (Ctrl+E)	🔎 ← → Search Depth: 3 ▾
Name	**Value**
RSP,X	0x00000074F22FF9C0
RIP,X	0x00007FF612B41020
RAX	8
Add item to watch	

6 See the instruction pointer address decrease as it now points to the earlier address of the custom procedure

7 See the custom procedure execute its instruction to clear the **RAX** register

Watch 1	▼ ↳ ×
Search (Ctrl+E)	🔎 ← → Search Depth: 3 ▾
Name	**Value**
RSP,X	0x00000074F22FF9C0
RIP,X	0x00007FF612B41023
RAX	0
Add item to watch	

8 Finally, see the **RET** instruction pop the stored address off the stack to return to the **main** procedure at that address

Watch 1	▼ ↳ ×
Search (Ctrl+E)	🔎 ← → Search Depth: 3 ▾
Name	**Value**
RSP,X	0x00000074F22FF9C8
RIP,X	0x00007FF612B41030
RAX	0
Add item to watch	

ASM

ARGS

Passing Register Arguments

Custom procedures often need to perform one or more tasks on argument values passed from the caller. High-level programming languages, such as C++, define functions with parameters to receive argument values, but in Assembly language programming you can simply reference argument values that have been assigned to registers. For example, a procedure to total the value of all elements in an array needs to be passed the starting array memory address and the array length as arguments – via two registers:

1 Create a new project named "ARGS" from the **MASM Template**, then open the **Source.asm** file

2 In the .**DATA** section of the file, declare and initialize an array variable of quad word size elements
arr QWORD 100, 150, 250

3 In the .**CODE main** procedure, assign the array length and its memory address to two registers
MOV RCX, LENGTHOF arr
LEA RDX, arr

4 Now, add a call to a custom procedure named "sum"
CALL sum

5 Before the **main** procedure in the .**CODE** section of the file, insert a custom procedure that contains a loop to add each element to a register and decrement a loop counter
```
sum PROC
XOR RAX, RAX
start:
ADD RAX, [ RDX ]
ADD RDX, 8
DEC RCX
JNZ start
RET
sum ENDP
```

The array memory address is incremented by eight on each iteration because the array elements are each quad word size.

6 Set a breakpoint, run the code and click **Step Into** to see the custom procedure add the elements via two registers

...cont'd

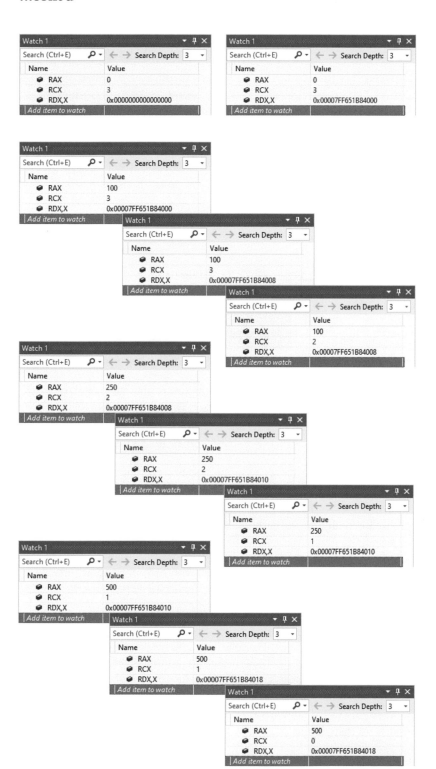

Passing Stack Arguments

As an alternative to passing arguments to a custom procedure via registers, as demonstrated in the previous example, arguments can be passed via the stack. It is, however, important to remember that a **CALL** instruction also pushes the return memory address onto the stack. This must be taken into account when trying to reference argument values pushed onto the stack in a procedure that subsequently calls a custom procedure. For example, pushing two quad word argument values onto the stack then calling a custom procedure means that the stack could look like this:

Address		
28h		
30h		
38h	**Return Address**	RSP
40h	**Argument 2**	RSP+8
48h	**Argument 1**	RSP+16

The custom procedure could first pop the return address from the stack into a register, then pop off each of the argument values to perform its operations on them. It would then need to push the return address back onto the stack before its final **RET** instruction.

Alternatively, the argument values can be referenced via the stack pointer. Recalling that the stack addresses decrease, each previous item added onto the stack can be referenced by adding its size (eight, for quad words) to the **RSP** register stack pointer.

The **RET** instruction will pop the return address off the stack when it returns to the procedure that made the call, but the argument values will still remain on the stack. In order to balance the stack once more, the argument values could be popped off into registers. This would, however, overwrite any existing values in those registers so is not desirable. The **POP** instruction doesn't actually remove items from the stack, it merely changes the location to which the **RSP** register points. This means the stack can be rebalanced simply by adding an appropriate number to the stack pointer. For example, with two quad word items remaining on the stack, the instruction **ADD RSP, 16** will rebalance the stack.

The return address is always 64-bit, so the first argument below it will always be **RSP+8**. The offset for a subsequent argument below that will depend on the size of the first argument. If it is a 16-bit word, the offset would be **RSP+10**.

1 Create a new project named "PARAMS" from the **MASM Template**, then open the **Source.asm** file

PARAMS

2 In the **.CODE main** procedure, clear a register then add argument values onto the stack
XOR RAX, RAX
PUSH 100
PUSH 500

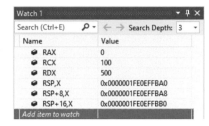

3 Next, add a call to a custom procedure named "max"
CALL max

4 Before the **main** procedure in the **.CODE** section of the file, insert a custom procedure that compares the arguments and copies the larger value into a register
max PROC
MOV RCX, [RSP+16]
MOV RDX, [RSP+8]
CMP RCX, RDX
JG large
MOV RAX, RDX
JMP finish
large:
MOV RAX, RCX
finish:
RET
max ENDP

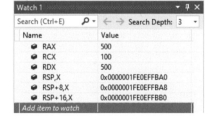

5 Now, return to the **main** procedure and add a final instruction to rebalance the stack
ADD RSP, 16

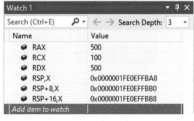

6 Set a breakpoint, run the code and click **Step Into** to see the custom procedure find the larger argument value

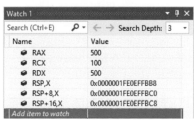

Using Local Scope

Variables defined in the **.DATA** section of an Assembly program are accessible from any procedure in the program. These persist all the time the program is running and are said to have "global scope".

Variables can, however, be created within a procedure that are only accessible from inside that procedure. These only exist until the procedure returns to the calling procedure, and have "local scope".

The region in memory allocated for the components needed by a procedure is called the "stack frame". This can be extended to allocate additional space for local variables. The **RBP** register contains the base address of the stack frame, and each item within the stack frame can be referenced as an offset to that base address.

To create local variables, the **RBP** base pointer must first be pushed onto the stack for storage, then the **RSP** stack pointer copied into the **RBP** base pointer to establish the base location. The **RSP** register can then be decremented to allocate space for the local variables. For example, where a procedure pushes one argument onto the stack before calling another procedure that reserves space for two local quad word size variables, the stack frame operation looks like this:

Don't forget

These offsets are all for 64-bit values. If the local variables are 16-bit, the offset would be **RBP-2**, **RBP-4**, etc.

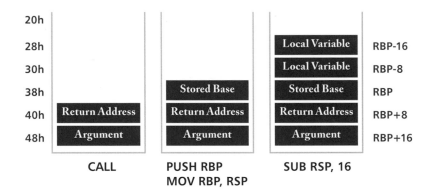

When a procedure has no further need of its local variables, the stack frame is no longer required, so the **RBP** base pointer must be copied back into the **RSP** stack pointer register, to restore the stack, and the **RBP** base pointer must be popped off the stack to restore the base pointer.

The **RBP** base pointer is set at a fixed location when using a stack frame, but the **RSP** stack pointer acts as usual.

1 Create a new project named "FRAME" from the **MASM Template**, then open the **Source.asm** file

ASM

FRAME

2 In the **.CODE main** procedure, clear a register, add an argument value onto the stack, then call a procedure
XOR RAX, RAX
PUSH 100
CALL total
ADD RSP, 8

Don't forget

Remember to finally rebalance the stack.

3 Before the **main** procedure in the **.CODE** section of the file, insert a custom procedure that uses the stack frame to allocate space for two local quad word size variables
total PROC
PUSH RBP
MOV RBP, RSP
SUB RSP, 16

MOV RSP, RBP
POP RBP
RET
max ENDP

Watch 1	▼ ᄆ ×
Search (Ctrl+E) 🔎 ▾ ← → Search Depth: 3 ▾	
Name	Value
● RBP+16,X	0x0000004852D4FD40
● RBP+8,X	0x0000004852D4FD38
● RBP,X	0x0000004852D4FD30
● RBP-8,X	0x0000004852D4FD28
● RBP-16,X	0x0000004852D4FD20
● RAX	0
Add item to watch	

4 Now, inside the stack frame, copy the argument value into local variables and total them all in a register
MOV RAX, [RBP+16]
MOV [RBP-8], RAX
MOV [RBP-16], RAX
ADD RAX, [RBP-8]
ADD RAX, [RBP-16]

5 Set a breakpoint, run the code and click **Step Into** to see the custom procedure use local variables

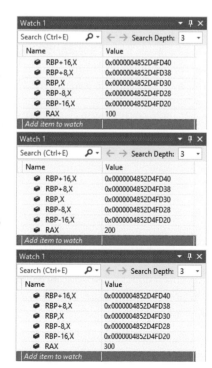

Watch 1	▼ ᄆ ×
Search (Ctrl+E) 🔎 ▾ ← → Search Depth: 3 ▾	
Name	Value
● RBP+16,X	0x0000004852D4FD40
● RBP+8,X	0x0000004852D4FD38
● RBP,X	0x0000004852D4FD30
● RBP-8,X	0x0000004852D4FD28
● RBP-16,X	0x0000004852D4FD20
● RAX	100
Add item to watch	

Watch 1	▼ ᄆ ×
Search (Ctrl+E) 🔎 ▾ ← → Search Depth: 3 ▾	
Name	Value
● RBP+16,X	0x0000004852D4FD40
● RBP+8,X	0x0000004852D4FD38
● RBP,X	0x0000004852D4FD30
● RBP-8,X	0x0000004852D4FD28
● RBP-16,X	0x0000004852D4FD20
● RAX	200
Add item to watch	

Watch 1	▼ ᄆ ×
Search (Ctrl+E) 🔎 ▾ ← → Search Depth: 3 ▾	
Name	Value
● RBP+16,X	0x0000004852D4FD40
● RBP+8,X	0x0000004852D4FD38
● RBP,X	0x0000004852D4FD30
● RBP-8,X	0x0000004852D4FD28
● RBP-16,X	0x0000004852D4FD20
● RAX	300
Add item to watch	

Calling Recursively

Assembly **CALL** instructions can freely call custom procedures just as readily as they can call Windows library functions, such as the **ExitProcess** instruction imported from the **kernel32.lib** library. Additionally, custom procedures can call themselves "recursively".

As with loops, it is important that recursive procedure calls must modify a tested value to avoid continuous execution – so the procedure will return at some point.

Recursive procedure calls can be used to emulate loop structures, such as the counting example on page 73. Additionally, they are useful to resolve mathematical problems such as the calculation of Fibonacci numbers, which has this formula:

$$F(n) = F(n-1) + F(n-2)$$

and produces this result:

1, 2, 3, 5, 8, 13, 21, 34, 55, 89, 144 etc.

This is simply a sequence of numbers in which each number after the second number is the total sum of the previous two numbers.

In Assembly programming, the Fibonacci sequence can be produced using only two registers. These are initialized with **1** and **0** respectively, then repeatedly exchanged and added together. This can be achieved using an **XCHG** instruction followed by an **ADD** instruction, or with one simple **XADD** instruction that combines the two stages. The **XADD** instruction has this syntax:

XADD   *Destination , Source*

- **Destination** – a register name if the source is a memory variable or another register, or a memory variable if the source is a register.

- **Source** – a register name if the destination is a memory variable or another register, or a memory variable if the destination is a register.

This first places the source value into the destination, and places the destination value into the source. It then adds the two together, placing the result in the destination location.

Italian mathematician Leonardo Bonacci (a.k.a. Fibonacci, c.1170-1240) was considered to be the most talented mathematician of the Middle Ages.

...cont'd

1 Create a new project named "RECUR" from the **MASM Template**, then open the **Source.asm** file

RECUR

2 In the **.CODE main** procedure, initialize two registers then call a procedure to produce Fibonacci numbers
MOV RAX, 1
MOV RDX, 1
CALL fib

3 Before the **main** procedure in the **.CODE** section of the file, insert a recursive procedure that will only return when a compared register value has been exceeded
fib PROC
; Add instructions here.
CMP RAX, 5
JG finish
CALL fib
finish:
RET
fib ENDP

Watch 1	▾ ꜔ ×
Search (Ctrl+E) 🔎 ▾ ← → Search Depth: 3 ▾	
Name	Value
● RCX	0
● RDX	1
● RAX	1
Add item to watch	

Watch 1	▾ ꜔ ×
Search (Ctrl+E) 🔎 ▾ ← → Search Depth: 3 ▾	
Name	Value
● RCX	1
● RDX	1
● RAX	2
Add item to watch	

Watch 1	▾ ꜔ ×
Search (Ctrl+E) 🔎 ▾ ← → Search Depth: 3 ▾	
Name	Value
● RCX	1
● RDX	2
● RAX	3
Add item to watch	

4 Now, inside the recursive procedure, add an instruction simply to display <u>both</u> previous numbers then exchange and add two registers
MOV RCX, RDX
XADD RAX, RDX

Watch 1	▾ ꜔ ×
Search (Ctrl+E) 🔎 ▾ ← → Search Depth: 3 ▾	
Name	Value
● RCX	2
● RDX	3
● RAX	5
Add item to watch	

Don't forget

Remember that the **MOV** instruction in Step 5 is not required to produce the Fibonacci sequence.

5 Set a breakpoint at the **CMP** instruction, then run the code and repeatedly click **Continue** to see the Fibonacci sequence produced by recursive calling

Watch 1	▾ ꜔ ×
Search (Ctrl+E) 🔎 ▾ ← → Search Depth: 3 ▾	
Name	Value
● RCX	3
● RDX	5
● RAX	8
Add item to watch	

Summary

- Procedures are small pieces of code that each perform a particular task, making the code easier to understand.

- When a procedure is implemented, the necessary information is saved on the stack data structure.

- Items can be added onto the top of the stack by a **PUSH** instruction, or removed from there by a **POP** instruction.

- The memory address of the top of the stack grows down as items are added to the stack.

- The **PUSH** and **POP** instructions must be used in pairs to avoid unbalancing the stack.

- The **RSP** register points to the top of the stack.

- Procedure blocks begin with a name and **PROC** directive, and end with a **RET** instruction then the name and **ENDP** directive.

- Procedures are implemented by a **CALL** instruction, which places the caller's address onto the stack.

- The **RET** instruction pops the caller's address off the stack as it returns to the next instruction after the **CALL** instruction.

- Arguments can be passed to procedures via registers or via the stack.

- Arguments on the stack can be referenced by adding an offset value to the **RSP** register stack pointer.

- The stack can be rebalanced by adding an appropriate number to the **RSP** register stack pointer.

- The **RBP** register points to the base address of the stack frame.

- Local variable space is created by decrementing the **RSP** stack pointer, after the **RBP** register has been stored on the stack.

- Local variables can be referenced by adding an offset value to the **RBP** register stack frame pointer.

- Procedures can call themselves recursively to perform loops.

- The **xadd** instruction first exchanges destination with source values, then places their sum total in the destination.

8 Expanding Macros

Injecting Text Items

A "macro" is a named block of text that can be injected into an Assembly program by the assembler. As it evaluates each line of code, it will recognize the name of a previously defined macro and replace the macro name at that location with the macro text.

With Assembly, you can define one-line macros, to insert a simple text string, and multi-line macros containing one or more statements. These enable you to avoid tediously writing the same code at several places throughout a program.

A one-line macro is created using a **TEXTEQU** directive that assigns a "text item" to a name of your choice. The **TEXTEQU** directive has this syntax:

Name	**TEXTEQU** < *Text* >

- **Name** – a symbolic name given to a text string.

- **Text** – a text string enclosed within < > angled brackets.

The substitution of macro text for the macro name is referred to as "macro expansion". It is important to recognize that macro expansion is a <u>text</u> substitution.

A multi-line macro is created using **MACRO** and **ENDM** (end macro) directives, which assign a text item to a name of your choice. The **MACRO** and **ENDM** directives have this syntax:

Name	**MACRO**
Text	
ENDM	

- **Name** – a symbolic name given to a text block.

- **Text** – a text block that can be one or many statements.

Macros are defined before the **.DATA** section of an Assembly program. Once defined, a macro can be called anywhere in the program simply by stating its name in the **.CODE** section of the program.

The Disassembly window in the Visual Studio IDE can be used to examine the macro text substitution.

114

Don't forget

Wherever a macro name appears in an Assembly program, the assembler will replace the macro's name by its text content.

MACRO

1   Create a new project named "MACRO" from the
    MASM Template, then open the **Source.asm** file

2   Before the .**DATA** section of the file, add a one-line macro
    to clear a register
    clrRAX TEXTEQU <XOR RAX, RAX>

3   Next, add a multi-line macro to clear another register
    clrRCX MACRO
    XOR RCX, RCX
    ENDM

4   In the .**CODE main** procedure, add statements to expand
    each macro
    clrRAX
    clrRCX

5   Set a breakpoint at the end of the .**CODE** section

6   Now, run the code to see the registers get cleared

Watch 1	▼ ₽ ×
Search (Ctrl+E) 🔎 ▾ ← → Search Depth: 3 ▾	
Name	Value
RAX	140696460726277
RCX	223062548480
Add item to watch	

Watch 1	▼ ₽ ×
Search (Ctrl+E) 🔎 ▾ ← → Search Depth: 3 ▾	
Name	Value
RAX	0
RCX	0
Add item to watch	

7   Click **Debug**, **Windows**, **Disassembly** to see the macros'
    text expanded into instructions at memory locations

Hot tip

Click the **Viewing
Options** arrow button
then choose the details
you want to see.

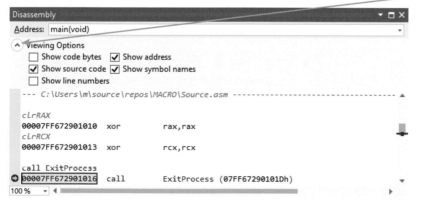

```
Disassembly                                               ▼ □ ×
Address:  main(void)                                           ▾
⌃ Viewing Options
    ☐ Show code bytes   ☑ Show address
    ☑ Show source code  ☑ Show symbol names
    ☐ Show line numbers
--- C:\Users\m\source\repos\MACRO\Source.asm ----------------- ▲

clrRAX
00007FF672901010  xor        rax,rax
clrRCX
00007FF672901013  xor        rcx,rcx

call ExitProcess
⬤ 00007FF672901016  call       ExitProcess (07FF67290101Dh)  ▾
100 %  ▾ ◀                                                  ▶
```

Adding Parameters

Parameters can be added to a multi-line macro definition to make it more flexible by allowing the caller to pass arguments to the macro. A parameter name of your choice is simply added after the **MACRO** directive, or multiple parameter names can be added there as a comma-separated list:

> *Name*   **MACRO**   *Parameter1 , Parameter2 , Parameter3*
>
> *Statements-to-be-executed*
>
> **ENDM**

Macros are passed arguments from the caller in the **.CODE** section of the program by adding the argument value after the macro's name, or multiple argument values are added there as a comma-separated list. The number of arguments must match the number of parameters, but you can explicitly enforce the requirement of any parameter by adding a **:REQ** suffix to the parameter name:

> *Name*   **MACRO**   *Parameter1***:REQ** *, Parameter2*
>
> *Statements-to-be-executed*
>
> **ENDM**

Allowance can made for missing arguments, however, by specifying default values for any parameter. The value is specified following a := suffix to the parameter name. Recalling that macros are "text items", you can only specify a numeric default value as a text string by enclosing it within < > angled brackets. For example, to assign the text string number eight, like this:

> *Name*   **MACRO**   *Parameter1***:REQ** *, Parameter2***:=<8>**
>
> *Statements-to-be-executed*
>
> **ENDM**

Parameters that specify a default value should be at the end of the parameter list, as passed arguments get assigned to the parameters in left-to-right order.

MARGS

1 Create a new project named "MARGS" from the **MASM Template**, then open the **Source.asm** file

2 Before the **.DATA** section of the file, add a macro to clear the register specified by an argument passed from the caller
clrReg MACRO reg
XOR reg, reg
ENDM

3 Next, add a macro to assign the total of two parameter values to a specified register
sum MACRO reg:REQ, x:=<2>, y:=<8>
MOV reg, x
ADD reg, y
ENDM

4 In the **.CODE main** procedure, add a statement to expand the first macro
clrReg RAX

5 Then, add statements to expand the second macro using default and supplied argument values
sum RBX
sum RBX, 12
sum RBX,18,12

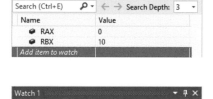

6 Set a breakpoint, then run the code and click **Step Into**

7 Examine the Watch window to see the instructions executed after the macro substitutions

117

Making Decisions

Within macros, an **IF** directive can be used to perform the basic conditional test that evaluates a given expression for a boolean value of true or false. Statements following the evaluation will only be executed when the expression's condition is found to be true. The condition can be tested using these relational operators:

EQ	Equal
NE	Not Equal
GT	Greater Than
LT	Less Than
GE	Greater or Equal
LE	Less or Equal

There may be one or more statements, but the **IF** block must end with an **ENDIF** directive, so the **IF** block syntax looks like this:

```
IF Test-Expression

        Statements-to-execute-when-the-condition-is-true
ENDIF
```

Hot tip

An **IF**-**ENDIF** block can also be nested within an outer **IF**-**ENDIF** block to test multiple conditions.

An **IF** block can, optionally, provide alternative statements to only be executed when the expression's condition is found to be false by including an **ELSE** directive, like this:

```
IF Test-Expression

        Statements-to-execute-when-the-condition-is-true
ELSE

        Statements-to-execute-when-the-condition-is-false
ENDIF
```

Additionally, a macro can test more than one condition in an **IF** block by including an **ELSEIF** directive, using this syntax:

```
IF First-Test-Expression

        Statements-to-execute-when-the-first-condition-is-true
ELSEIF Second-Test-Expression

        Statements-to-execute-when-the-second-condition-is-true
ELSE

        Statements-to-execute-when-both-conditions-are-false
ENDIF
```

...cont'd

MIF

1 Create a new project named "MIF" from the **MASM Template**, then open the **Source.asm** file

2 Before the **.DATA** section of the file, begin a macro to assign a value to a register if the passed argument exceeds 50

```
scan MACRO num
IF num GT 50
MOV RAX, 1
```

3 Next, in the macro, assign a value to a register if the passed argument is below 50

```
ELSEIF num LT 50
MOV RAX, 0
```

4 Now, in the macro, assign a value to a register if the passed argument is exactly 50

```
ELSE
MOV RAX, num
```

5 Complete the macro by terminating the **IF** block and the entire macro block

```
ENDIF
ENDM
```

6 In the **.CODE main** procedure, add statements to call the macro to examine three different argument values

```
scan 100
scan 0
scan 50
```

7 Set a breakpoint, then run the code and click **Step Into**

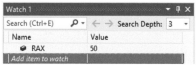

8 Examine the Watch window to see the macro assign appropriate register values for each passed argument

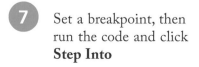

Hot tip

An **IF-ENDIF** block, and similar conditional tests and loops in this chapter, can appear in the **.code** section, but the examples in this chapter demonstrate these structures within macros.

Repeating Loops

Macro blocks can contain other macros, and this is especially useful to include unnamed macros that repeatedly execute their statements in a loop.

The **REPEAT** loop directive executes its statements for a specified number of iterations. The **REPEAT** block is itself a macro so must end with an **ENDM** directive. The **REPEAT** block has this syntax:

> **REPEAT** *Number-of-Iterations*
>
> *Statements-to-be-executed-on-each-iteration*
>
> **ENDM**

The **WHILE** loop directive evaluates a given expression for a boolean value of true or false and executes its statements while the condition remains true. The expression typically uses the relational operators **GT**, **LT**, etc. but it can be an expression that evaluates to any non-zero value (true) or to zero (false).

The **WHILE** block is itself a macro so must end with an **ENDM** directive. The **WHILE** block has this syntax:

> **WHILE** *Test-Expression*
>
> *Statements-to-be-executed-on-each-iteration*
>
> **ENDM**

A loop block within a macro can include a conditional test to break out of the loop by implementing an **EXITM** (exit macro) directive if a tested condition becomes false. This is incorporated as the sole statement to be executed within an **IF** block, like this:

> **WHILE** *Test-Expression*
>
> **IF** *Test-Expression*
>
> **EXITM**
>
> **ENDIF**
>
> *Statements-to-be-executed-on-each-iteration*
>
> **ENDM**

The **MOD** operator can be used to determine whether a number is even or odd, by combining it with the **EQ** relational operator to test if the remainder is zero after division by two.

If the test expression evaluates to false when first tested, the loop will end immediately without executing any statements.

1 Create a new project named "MRPT" from the **MASM Template**, then open the **Source.asm** file

ASM

MRPT

2 Before the **.DATA** section of the file, add a macro to repeatedly increment a specified register a specified number of times
```
rpt MACRO reg, num
        REPEAT num
        INC reg
        ENDM
ENDM
```

3 Next, add a macro to repeatedly increment a specified register until a specified limit is reached
```
itr MACRO reg, num
        count = num
        WHILE count LE 100
        count = count + 27
        MOV reg, count
        ; Test to be inserted here.
        ENDM
ENDM
```

4 Now, in the macro, insert a test to exit the loop if the counter value becomes an even number
```
IF count MOD 2 EQ 0
EXITM
ENDIF
```

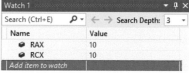

5 In the **.CODE main** procedure, add statements to initialize two registers, then call the macros to loop
```
MOV RAX, 10
MOV RCX, 10
rpt RAX, 10
itr RCX, 10
```

6 Set a breakpoint, then run the code and click **Step Into**

7 Examine the Watch window to see the macros assign values

Iterating Loops

In addition to the loops that repeat blocks of statements, as demonstrated by the previous example, a macro can contain a loop that iterates through a list of arguments, executing a task on each argument in turn.

The **FOR** directive executes its statements on each argument in a specified list. The arguments are represented in turn by a named parameter specified to the **FOR** directive. The **FOR** block is itself a macro so must end with an **ENDM** directive, and has this syntax:

```
FOR  Parameter-Name , < Argument-List >
         Statements-to-be-executed-on-each-argument
ENDM
```

The parameter name is one you choose, following the usual naming conventions, and the arguments list is a comma-separated list that must be enclosed within **< >** angled brackets.

On the first iteration, the parameter name references the value of the first list argument; on the second iteration the parameter name references the second list argument, and so on.

There is a similar **FORC** directive that executes its statements on each character in a specified string. The characters are represented in turn by a named parameter specified to the **FORC** directive. The **FORC** block is itself a macro, so must end with an **ENDM** directive and has this syntax:

```
FORC  Parameter-Name , < Text >
         Statements-to-be-executed-on-each-character
ENDM
```

In order to directly reference the character represented by the parameter name it is necessary to enclose the parameter name within quote marks and prefix the parameter name with an **&** ampersand character. In this case, the **&** acts as a substitution operator to ensure that the value is expanded to a character, rather than be regarded as a literal string.

Hot tip

The **< >** angled brackets enable the argument list or text content to be treated as a single literal element, through which the loop can iterate over each item.

...cont'd

ASM

MFOR

1 Create a new project named "MFOR" from the **MASM Template**, then open the **Source.asm** file

2 Before the **.DATA** section of the file, add a macro to push a number onto the stack on each iteration of a loop, then pop each number into a register

```
nums MACRO arg1, arg2, arg3
        FOR arg, < arg1, arg2, arg3 >
        PUSH arg
        ENDM
POP RCX
POP RBX
POP RAX
ENDM
```

3 Next, in the **.DATA** section, add a macro to push a character onto the stack on each iteration of a loop, then pop each character into a register

```
chars MACRO arglist
        FORC arg, arglist
        PUSH '&arg'
        ENDM
POP RCX
POP RBX
POP RAX
ENDM
```

4 In the **.CODE main** procedure, add statements to call the macros, passing three numeric arguments and a string of three characters respectively

```
nums 1, 2, 3
chars <ABC>
```

5 Set a breakpoint, then run the code and click **Step Into**

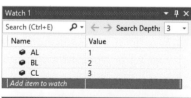

6 Examine the Watch window to see the macro loops assign values

Attaching Labels

Labels can be included within macros as jump targets, but a label can only be defined once in the program source code. Calling a macro that includes labels more than once would expand the macro each time and therefore produce symbol redefinition errors.

The solution to avoid symbol redefinition errors is to declare each label name using a **LOCAL** directive on the first line inside the macro body. MASM will then generate internal names at different addresses each time the macro is called.

MLBL

1 Create a new project named "MLBL" from the **MASM Template**, then open the **Source.asm** file

2 Before the **.DATA** section of the file, add a macro with labels to raise a specified base number to a specified power
```
power MACRO base:REQ, exponent:REQ
; LOCAL directive to be inserted here.
MOV RAX, 1
MOV RCX, exponent
CMP RCX, 0
JE finish
MOV RBX, base
start:
MUL RBX
LOOP start
finish:
ENDM
```

3 Next, in the **.CODE main** procedure, add statements to call the macro twice
```
power 4,2
power 4,3
```

The **Error List** window should automatically appear, or you can click **View**, **Error List** on the menu bar to open it.

4 Set a breakpoint, then run the code and see the build fail with symbol redefinition errors

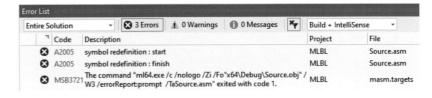

5 Now, insert a **LOCAL** directive on the first line of the macro body, to define local labels
LOCAL start, finish

6 Run the code and see the build now succeeds, then click **Step Into** to see the macros execute their statements

7 Remain in Debug mode and click **Debug, Windows, Disassembly** on the Visual Studio toolbar – to open the "Disassembly" window

8 See that the generated internal name addresses differ each time the macro was called

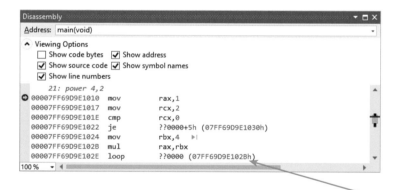

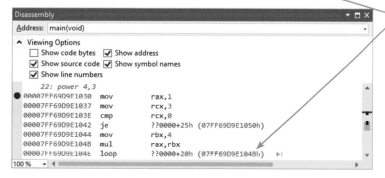

Internal name address for start.

Returning Values

A macro can return a text value to the caller simply by appending the return value after the **EXITM** directive. Macros that do return a value are also referred to as "macro functions".

Macro functions are called like other macros, but arguments must be enclosed in **( )** parentheses. Where the return value is numeric, it can be converted into a text item by enclosing the value in **< >** angled brackets.

A macro function could, for instance, return the factorial of a specified number – the sum of all positive integers less than or equal to the specified number.

MRTN

1 Create a new project named "MRTN" from the **MASM Template**, then open the **Source.asm** file

2 Before the **.DATA** section of the file, add a macro to return the factorial of a passed argument value
```
factorial MACRO num:REQ
factor = num
i = 1
        WHILE factor GT 1
        i = i * factor
        factor = factor - 1
        ENDM
EXITM < i >
ENDM
```

3 Next, in the **.CODE main** procedure, add statements to call the macro twice
```
MOV RAX, factorial( 4 )
MOV RBX, factorial( 5 )
```

The returned text item is stored in binary format within registers so can subsequently be treated as a number.

4 Set a breakpoint, then run the code and click **Step Into** to see the returned factorial values

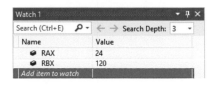

Varying Argument List

A macro can accept a varying number of arguments by adding a :**VARARG** suffix to a parameter name. There may be other parameters defined but you can only suffix :**VARARG** to the final parameter. This nominates the final parameter name to represent all additional arguments.

Name	**MACRO** *Param1*:**REQ** , *Param2*:**=<8>** , *Param3*:**VARARG**
	Statements-to-be-executed
	ENDM

Typically, a **FOR** loop can be created to process the arguments, irrespective of the quantity.

1 Create a new project named "MVAR" from the **MASM Template**, then open the **Source.asm** file

ASM

MVAR

2 Before the .**DATA** section of the file, add a macro to count the number of arguments and return their sum total

```
sumArgs MACRO arglist:VARARG
sum = 0
i = 0
        FOR arg, < arglist >
        i = i + 1
        sum = sum + arg
        ENDM
MOV RCX, i
EXITM < sum >
ENDM
```

3 Next, in the .**CODE main** procedure, add statements to call the macro twice

```
MOV RAX, sumArgs( 1, 2, 3, 4 )
MOV RAX, sumArgs( 1, 2, 3, 4, 5, 6, 7, 8 )
```

4 Set breakpoints after each call, then run the code and click **Continue** to see the sum and count of the passed argument values

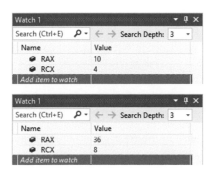

Summary

- The Assembler will replace a macro name in a program with the text contained within the macro of that name.

- The **TEXTEQU** directive assigns a text item to a name, to create a one-line macro.

- The **MACRO** and **ENDM** directives assign a text block to a name, to create a multi-line macro.

- Parameters can be added to a multi-line macro definition, so that arguments can be passed to the macro from the caller.

- A parameter :**REQ** suffix enforces requirement of an argument, and a := suffix can specify a default value.

- The **IF** and **ENDIF** directives create a conditional test block that evaluates an expression for a boolean value of true or false.

- The relational operators **EQ, NE, GT, LT, GE** and **LE** compare two operands and return a true or false condition result.

- Alternative statements can be provided within an **IF** block by including **ELSE** and **ELSEIF** directives.

- The **REPEAT** and **ENDM** directives create a block that executes its statements a specified number of times.

- The **WHILE** and **ENDM** directives create a block that repeatedly executes its statements while a tested condition remains true.

- The **EXITM** directive exits a macro block and can be used to return a text value to the caller from a macro function.

- The **FOR** and **ENDM** directives create a block that iterates through each item in a specified argument list.

- The **FORC** and **ENDM** directives create a block that iterates through each character in a specified text string.

- Labels within a macro should be declared on the first line to a **LOCAL** directive, to avoid symbol redefinition errors.

- When calling a macro function, the caller must enclose the arguments it is passing within ( ) parentheses.

- A final parameter :**VARARG** suffix allows a varying number of arguments to be passed to a macro.

9 Floating Points

Streaming Extensions

Modern CPUs incorporate enhancements to the basic x86 instruction set to provide Single Instruction Multiple Data (SIMD) capability and support for floating-point arithmetic.

SIMD has special instructions that can greatly improve performance when the same operation is to be performed on multiple items of data. Intel first introduced Streaming SIMD Extensions (SSE), which added 128-bit registers to the CPU. Those instructions were extended with SSE2, SSE3, and SSE4. Then, Advanced Vector Extensions (AVX) first added 256-bit registers, and later AVX-512 added 512-bit registers. The SSE and AVX enhancements are also available on AMD CPUs, but not all versions of either manufacturer's products have all the extensions.

The free Intel® Processor Identification Utility program can be used to discover which extensions are available on your CPU. At the time of writing, you can download this for Windows from **downloadcenter.intel.com/download/28539/Intel-Processor-Identification-Utility-Windows-Version**

Alternatively, you can use the free CPU-Z utility program to discover which extensions are available on your AMD CPU. At the time of writing, you can download this for Windows from **www.cpuid.com/softwares/cpu-z.html**

The additional registers added by the CPU enhancements provide the following new features not previously available:

- **SIMD** – the same instruction performed simultaneously on multiple pairs of operands.

- **Floating Point** – supporting fractions and scientific notation.

- **Saturation Arithmetic** – filling result registers with highest (or lowest) value, instead of setting carry or overflow flags.

- **Special Instructions** – performing operations such as fused multiply/add (floating-point multiply and add in one step).

The SSE and AVX instructions use their own registers, which are separate from the general purpose 64-bit registers. The number of registers can, however, vary according to the CPU version:

- **XMM** – (8, 16, or 32) 128-bit registers for SSE instructions. Typically, 16 registers **XMM0** to **XMM15**.

- **YMM** – (16 or 32) 256-bit registers for AVX instructions. Typically, 16 registers **YMM0** to **YMM15**.

- **ZMM** – (32) 512-bit registers for AVX-512 instructions. **ZMM0** to **ZMM31**.

At the time of writing, AVX-512 is only supported by certain Intel CPUs.

The registers for each set of instructions overlap, so the lower 128 bits of the **YMM** registers are the same as the **XMM** registers. Similarly, the lower 256 bits of the **ZMM** registers are the same as the **YMM** registers, and the lower 128 bits of the **ZMM** registers are the same as the **XMM** registers.

ZMM 512-bits

YMM 256-bits

XMM 128-bits

As the SSE instruction set was introduced earlier than AVX, it's most likely to be available on your CPU, so the examples in this chapter will first demonstrate SSE instructions on the **XMM** registers, then move on to their AVX **YMM** equivalents.

Packing Lanes

Streaming SIMD Extensions (SSE) provide instructions to perform arithmetical operations. Unlike logical operations, which perform on individual bits in a fixed-size column, arithmetical operations need to expand to use more bits for 10s, 100s, etc.

To perform multiple simultaneous arithmetical operations, the SSE instructions "pack" arithmetical operations into fixed same-size "lanes" that allow for expansion, but do not allow results to spill over into other lanes. The number of lanes in the 128-bit XMM registers depend on the width of the lanes' data type:

Lane Width:	BYTE (8-bits)	WORD (16-bits)	DWORD (32-bits)	QWORD (64-bits)
No. of Lanes:	16	8	4	2

The SSE **MOVDQA** instruction is used to assign 128 bits of data to a register or to a memory variable, and has this syntax:

MOVDQA *Destination , Source*

- **Destination** – a register name, or a memory variable if the source is a register.

- **Source** – a register name, or a memory variable if the destination is a register.

Note that you cannot move data from memory to memory, nor can you assign immediate values as the source with SSE.

For SSE instructions, an **XMMWORD** data type represents 128 bits. This can be used with a **PTR** (pointer) directive to assign 128 bits of data to an **XMM** register. The operation has this syntax:

MOVDQA *Register-Name* , **XMMWORD PTR** [*Source*]

The SSE **PADDD** addition instruction is used to add the value in the source to the value in the destination, and has this syntax:

PADDD *Destination , Source*

- **Destination** – a register name.

- **Source** – a register name, or a memory variable.

Hot tip

The **MOVDQA** instruction assigns a double quad word – a 128-bit "octoword".

1 Create a new project named "SIMD" from the **MASM Template**, then open the **Source.asm** file

ASM

SIMD

2 In the .**DATA** section of the file, initialize two 128-bit variable arrays, each with four 32-bit elements
nums0 DWORD 1, 2, 3, 4
nums1 DWORD 1, 3, 5, 7

3 Next, in the .**CODE main** procedure, add a statement to assign the values in the first array to a register
MOVDQA XMM0, XMMWORD PTR [nums0]

4 Now, add a statement to add the values in the second array to those in the register
PADDD XMM0, XMMWORD PTR [nums1]

5 Set a breakpoint, then run the code and expand the register's icon in the Watch window to see the addition

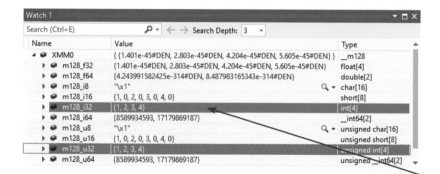

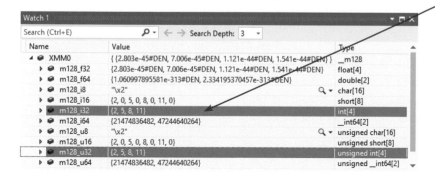

Parallel integer addition.

Aligning Data

The SSE instructions, like all Assembly instructions, are "mnemonics" – a pattern of letters describing the purpose of the instruction. The purpose of basic Assembly instructions, such as **ADD** or **MOV**, is quite obvious. The SSE instructions, such as **PADDD** or **MOVDQA**, also describe the data for the operation, so their purpose is less obvious. For example, **PADDD** means **P-ADD-D** (packed integer, add, double word). For subtraction there is also a **P-SUB-D** (packed integer, subtract, double word) instruction.

Similarly, **MOVDQA** means **MOV-DQ-A** (move, double quad word, aligned). So, what does "aligned" mean here?

Alignment

SSE requires its data to be aligned to 16-byte (128-bit) boundaries. Essentially, this simply requires the memory address of the data to be exactly divisible by 16. It is, however, something to be aware of when adding variables to the **.DATA** section of an Assembly program that will use SSE instructions, as execution can fail if the data is unaligned. For example, adding an 8-bit byte variable between a number of 32-bit double word variables would cause the later double word variables to be unaligned:

Data	Address	Decimal	Step	
nums0	0000h	(0)	0	DWORD 32-bits
nums1	0010h	(16)	16	DWORD 32-bits
var	0020h	(32)	16	BYTE 8-bits
nums2	0021h	(33)	8	DWORD 32-bits – Unaligned!
nums3	0031h	(49)	16	DWORD 32-bits – Unaligned!

There are alternative SSE instructions, such as **MOVDQU** (move, double quad word, unaligned) that sidestep this issue, but a better solution is to add an **ALIGN** directive into the variable list. This directive aligns the next item of data on an address that is a multiple of its parameter. In the case of a 16-byte boundary, as required by SSE instructions, placing an **ALIGN 16** directive into the variable list just before an unaligned variable will bring it back into alignment.

Avoid unaligned data when using SSE instructions.

1 Create a new project named "ALIGN" from the **MASM Template**, then open the **Source.asm** file

2 In the **.DATA** section of the file, initialize two 32-bit variable arrays, around a single-byte variable
nums0 DWORD 1, 2, 3, 4
snag BYTE 100
; Align directive to be inserted here.
nums1 DWORD 5, 5, 5, 5

3 Next, in the **.CODE main** procedure, add statements to assign the arrays to registers and perform subtractions
MOVDQA XMM0, XMMWORD PTR [nums0]
MOVDQA XMM1, XMMWORD PTR [nums1]
PSUBD XMM0, XMM1

4 Set a breakpoint, then run the code to see execution fail due to unaligned data

```
Source.asm  ⊣  ×
     10    .CODE
     11  ⊟main PROC
●    12    MOVDQA XMM0, XMMWORD PTR [nums0]
⇨    13    MOVDQA XMM1, XMMWORD PTR [nums1]   ⊗
     14    PSUBD XMM0, XMM1
     15
     16    CALL ExitProcess
     17    main ENDP
     18
     19    END
```

Exception Thrown   ⊣ ×

Exception thrown at 0x00007FF6B7351018 in ALIGN.exe: 0xC0000005:
Access violation reading location 0xFFFFFFFFFFFFFFFF.

Copy Details | Start Live Share session...
▷ Exception Settings

5 In the **.DATA** section of the file, insert a directive to align the second array
ALIGN 16

6 Run the code and expand the register's icon in the Watch window to see the subtraction result in negative integers

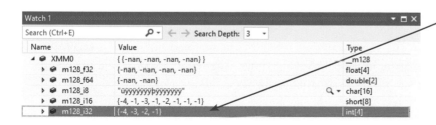

Negative integers.

```
Watch 1                                                          ▾ □ ×
Search (Ctrl+E)           𝒫 ▾  ← →  Search Depth: 3  ▾
Name                Value                              Type
▲ ● XMM0            {{-nan, -nan, -nan, -nan}}         _m128
  ▷ ● m128_f32      {-nan, -nan, -nan, -nan}           float[4]
  ▷ ● m128_f64      {-nan, -nan}                       double[2]
  ▷ ● m128_i8       "ÿÿÿÿÿÿÿÿÿbÿÿÿÿÿÿÿ"           Q ▾  char[16]
  ▷ ● m128_i16      {-4, -1, -3, -1, -2, -1, -1, -1}   short[8]
  ▷ ● m128_i32      {-4, -3, -2, -1}                   int[4]
```

Exacting Precision

Although SSE supports basic integer arithmetic, it is better suited for floating point arithmetic. Adhering to the IEEE (Institute of Electrical and Electronics Engineers) standard for floating-point arithmetic, the **XMM** registers can store floating point numbers in single-precision format, using 32 bits for each number, or in double-precision format using 64 bits for each number.

With the single-precision 32-bit (float) format, the Most Significant Bit is used to indicate whether the number is positive or negative. The following 8 bits are reserved for the exponent integer part of the number, and the final 23 bits are used for the fractional part of the number.

32-bit = float, single precision

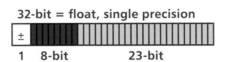

1   8-bit   23-bit

With the double-precision 64-bit (double) format, the Most Significant Bit is used to indicate whether the number is positive or negative. The following 11 bits are reserved for the exponent integer part of the number, and the final 52 bits are used for the fractional part of the number.

64-bit = double, double precision

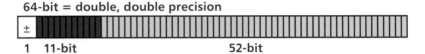

1   11-bit   52-bit

Double floating-point precision is used where a greater degree of precision is needed, but as it requires more memory, single precision is more widely used for normal calculations.

For SSE single precision, 32-bit floating-point numbers can be declared as variables of the **REAL4** data type, which allocates four bytes of memory, and double-precision 64-bit floating-point numbers can be declared of the **REAL8** data type which allocates eight bytes of memory.

The floating-point numbers can be assigned to **XMM** registers in the same way that integers are assigned but using a **MOVAPS** instruction (**MOV-A-P-S** – move, aligned, packed, single precision) or a **MOVAPD** instruction (**MOV-A-P-D** – move, aligned, packed, double precision).

The 32-bit **REAL4** data type is just like the 32-bit **DWORD** data type, but interpreted in a different way – to recognize floating-point precision.

1 Create a new project named "PRECIS" from the **MASM Template**, then open the **Source.asm** file

PRECIS

2 In the **.DATA** section of the file, initialize two floating-point variable arrays
nums REAL4 1.5, 2.5, 3.5, 3.1416
dubs REAL8 1.5, 3.1415926535897932

3 Next, in the **.CODE main** procedure, add statements to assign the arrays to registers
MOVAPS XMM0, XMMWORD PTR [nums]
MOVAPD XMM1, XMMWORD PTR [dubs]

4 Set a breakpoint, then run the code and click **Step Into**

5 Examine the Watch window to see the single-precision floating-point numbers assigned

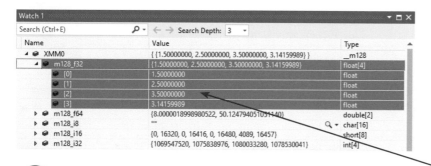

Single precision.

6 Click **Step Into** once more to see the double-precision floating-point numbers assigned

Double precision.

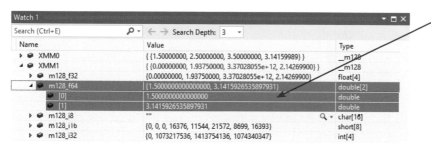

Handling Scalars

For operations on just one single number, SSE provides several unitary "scalar" instructions. Variables initialized with a single floating-point number can simply be assigned to an **XMM** register.

Variables of the **REAL4** 32-bit data type can be assigned using a **MOVSS** instruction (move, scalar, single precision) and variables of the **REAL8** 64-bit data type can be assigned using a **MOVSD** instruction (move, scalar, double precision). The assigned values will only occupy the first 32 or 64 bits of the **XMM** register respectively. These instructions have this syntax:

> **MOVSS** *Register-Name* , *Register/Variable-Name*
>
> **MOVSD** *Register-Name* , *Register/Variable-Name*

Similarly, there are several SSE instructions to perform arithmetical operations on unitary scalar values for both single-precision and double-precision floating-point numbers:

Instruction	
ADDSS *Register-Name* , *Register/Variable-Name*	Add
ADDSD *Register-Name* , *Register/Variable-Name*	
SUBSS *Register-Name* , *Register/Variable-Name*	Subtract
SUBSD *Register-Name* , *Register/Variable-Name*	
MULSS *Register-Name* , *Register/Variable-Name*	Multiply
MULSD *Register-Name* , *Register/Variable-Name*	
DIVSS *Register-Name* , *Register/Variable-Name*	Divide
DIVSD *Register-Name* , *Register/Variable-Name*	

Hot tip

Store a copy of the value in the first operand at another location before performing arithmetic if you need to preserve that value.

In each case, the arithmetical instructions place the result of the operation in the first operand. For example, with the instruction **DIVSS XMM0, XMM1**, the operation divides the number in the first operand **XMM0** by the number in the second operand **XMM1**, and places the result of the operation in **XMM0** – replacing the original value in the first operand.

With all SSE arithmetical operations, the original value contained in the first operand is overwritten by the result of the operation. For this reason, SSE instructions are said to be "destructive".

1 Create a new project named "SCALAR" from the **MASM Template**, then open the **Source.asm** file

SCALAR

2 In the **.DATA** section of the file, initialize two floating-point scalar variables
num REAL4 16.0
factor REAL4 2.5

3 Next, in the **.CODE main** procedure, add statements to assign the scalars to registers
MOVSS XMM0, num
MOVSS XMM1, factor

4 Now, add statements to perform addition and multiplication on the assigned register values
ADDSS XMM0, XMM1
MULSS XMM0, XMM1

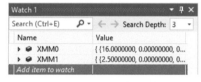

5 Then, add statements to perform subtraction and division on the assigned register values
SUBSS XMM0, XMM1
DIVSS XMM0, XMM1

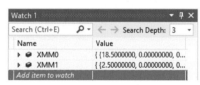

6 Set a breakpoint, then run the code and click **Step Into**

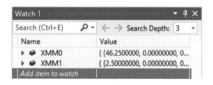

7 Examine the Watch window to see the value contained in the first register get repeatedly destroyed

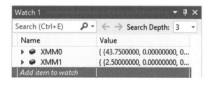

Handling Arrays

For simultaneous operations on multiple numbers, SSE provides several instructions for both single-precision and double-precision floating-point numbers. Variable arrays initialized with multiple floating-point numbers can be assigned to an **XMM** register with the **XMMWORD PTR [ ]** statement.

Variable arrays of the **REAL4** 32-bit data type can be assigned using the **MOVAPS** instruction (move, aligned, packed, single precision) and variable arrays of the **REAL8** 64-bit data type can be assigned using the **MOVAPD** instruction (move, aligned, packed, double precision). Remembering that the data must be aligned to 16-byte boundaries, the assigned values will occupy all 128 bits of the **XMM** register. These instructions have this syntax:

MOVAPS *Register-Name* , *Register/Variable-Name*
MOVAPD *Register-Name* , *Register/Variable-Name*

Similarly, there are several SSE instructions to perform simultaneous arithmetical operations on multiple values for both single-precision and double-precision floating-point numbers:

Instruction	
ADDPS *Register-Name* , *Register/Variable-Name*	Add
ADDPD *Register-Name* , *Register/Variable-Name*	
SUBPS *Register-Name* , *Register/Variable-Name*	Subtract
SUBPD *Register-Name* , *Register/Variable-Name*	
MULPS *Register-Name* , *Register/Variable-Name*	Multiply
MULPD *Register-Name* , *Register/Variable-Name*	
DIVPS *Register-Name* , *Register/Variable-Name*	Divide
DIVPD *Register-Name* , *Register/Variable-Name*	

In each case, the arithmetical instructions place the result of the operation in the first operand. For example, with the instruction **MULPS XMM0, XMM1**, the operation multiplies the number in the first operand **XMM0** by the number in the second operand **XMM1**, and places the result of the operation in **XMM0** – destroying the original value in the first operand.

The **MOVAPS** instruction requires an array of four single-precision numbers, and the **MOVAPD** instruction requires an array of two double-precision numbers.

SSE instructions are destructive.

1 Create a new project named "ARRAY" from the **MASM Template**, then open the **Source.asm** file

ARRAY

2 In the **.DATA** section of the file, initialize four floating-point array variables
nums REAL4 12.5, 25.0, 37.5, 50.0
numf REAL4 2.0, 3.0, 4.0, 5.0
dubs REAL8 12.5, 25.0
dubf REAL8 2.0, 3.0

3 Next, in the **.CODE main** procedure, add statements to assign the single-precision arrays to registers, then perform a division on each number
MOVAPS XMM0, XMMWORD PTR [nums]
MOVAPS XMM1, XMMWORD PTR [numf]
DIVPS XMM0, XMM1

4 Now, add statements to assign the double-precision arrays to registers, then perform a division on each number
MOVAPD XMM2, XMMWORD PTR [dubs]
MOVAPD XMM3, XMMWORD PTR [dubf]
DIVPD XMM2, XMM3

5 Set a breakpoint, then run the code and click **Step Into**

6 Examine the Watch window to see simultaneous arithmetical operations performed on the single-precision and double-precision array element values

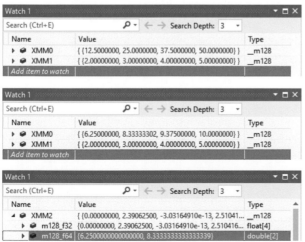

Saturating Ranges

SSE instructions that produce results outside the range of a container do not set the carry flag or overflow flag. You can, however, use "saturation arithmetic" to indicate when a problem has occurred with packed integer addition or subtraction.

Saturation arithmetic limits all operations to a fixed minimum and a fixed maximum value. If the result of an operation is greater than the maximum, it is set ("clamped") to the maximum. Conversely, if the result of an operation is less than the minimum, it is clamped to the minimum.

With SSE saturation arithmetic, the signed **SBYTE** data type has a result range of -128 to 127. If a result exceeds 127 using saturation arithmetic, the processor will present 127 as the result, or if a result is less than -128 using saturation arithmetic, the processor will present -128 as the result.

There are signed data types for each data size that add an **S** prefix to their unsigned counterparts; i.e. **SBYTE**, **SWORD**, **SDWORD**, and **SQWORD**. SSE provides saturation integer arithmetic instructions for both unsigned and signed data types:

Instruction	Operation
PADDUSB	Packed add unsigned **BYTE**
PSUBUSB	Packed subtract unsigned **BYTE**
PADDSB	Packed add signed **BYTE**
PSUBSB	Packed subtract signed **BYTE**
PADDUSW	Packed add unsigned **WORD**
PSUBUSW	Packed subtract unsigned **WORD**
PADDSW	Packed add signed **WORD**
PSUBSW	Packed subtract signed **WORD**
PADDUSD	Packed add unsigned **DWORD**
PSUBUSD	Packed subtract unsigned **DWORD**
PADDSD	Packed add signed **DWORD**
PSUBSD	Packed subtract signed **DWORD**
PADDUSQ	Packed add unsigned **QWORD**
PSUBUSQ	Packed subtract unsigned **QWORD**
PADDSQ	Packed add signed **QWORD**
PSUBSQ	Packed subtract signed **QWORD**

Hot tip

The **SWORD** data type has a result range of -32,768 to 32,767. If a result exceeds the upper limit, the processor will present 32,767 as the result, and if a result is below the lower limit, the processor will present -32,768 as the result.

1 Create a new project named "SATUR" from the **MASM Template**, then open the **Source.asm** file

SATUR

2 In the **.DATA** section of the file, initialize two 128-bit signed byte array variables
nums SBYTE 16 DUP (50)
tons SBYTE 16 DUP (100)

3 Next, in the **.CODE main** procedure, add statements to assign the first array to a register then perform addition of the second array values to each element
MOVAPS XMM0, XMMWORD PTR [nums]
PADDSB XMM0, tons

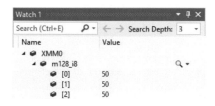 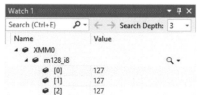

4 Now, add statements to assign the first array to a register once more, then perform successive subtraction of the second array values to each element
MOVAPS XMM0, XMMWORD PTR [nums]
PSUBSB XMM0, tons
PSUBSB XMM0, tons

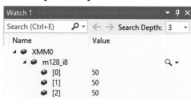

5 Set a breakpoint, then run the code and click **Step Into**

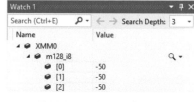

6 Examine the Watch window to see saturation arithmetic present 127 when the upper limit is exceeded, and present -128 when the lower limit is exceeded

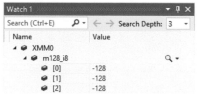

Using Specials

There are, quite literally, hundreds of instructions supported by the x64 CPU architecture. You can find a complete description of the entire instruction set in the Intel Developer's Manual available for free download from **software.intel.com**
It is comprehensive, but runs to over 2,000 pages!

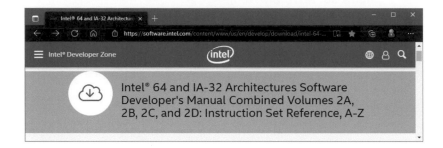

Some of the more common specialized instructions that perform useful calculations are listed in the table below:

144

The **XMM1** and **XMM2** registers are given here as examples, but any two **XMM** registers could be used for these calculations.

Instruction	Operation
MINSS	Minimum of scalar single-precision floating-point value between XMM1 and XMM2
MINPS	Minimum of packed single-precision floating-point value between XMM1 and XMM2
MINPD	Minimum of packed double-precision floating-point value between XMM1 and XMM2
MAXSS	Maximum of scalar single-precision floating-point value between XMM1 and XMM2
MAXPS	Maximum of packed single-precision floating-point value between XMM1 and XMM2
MAXPD	Maximum of packed double-precision floating-point value between XMM1 and XMM2
ROUNDSS	Round scalar single-precision floating-point value between XMM1 and XMM2
ROUNDPS	Round packed single-precision floating-point value between XMM1 and XMM2
ROUNDPD	Round packed double-precision floating-point value between XMM1 and XMM2
PAVGB	Average packed unsigned byte integers between XMM1 and XMM2
PAVGW	Average packed unsigned word integers between XMM1 and XMM2

...cont'd

1 Create a new project named "SPECS" from the **MASM Template**, then open the **Source.asm** file

ASM

SPECS

2 In the **.DATA** section of the file, initialize two arrays
```
nums1 REAL4 44.5, 58.25, 32.6, 19.8
nums2 REAL4 22.7, 73.2, 66.15, 12.3
```

3 Next, in the **.CODE main** procedure, add statements to assign the arrays to registers then place the highest value of each pair in the first register
```
MOVDQA XMM1, XMMWORD PTR [ nums1 ]
MOVDQA XMM2, XMMWORD PTR [ nums2 ]
MAXPS XMM1, XMM2
```

4 Now, add statements to place the lowest value of each pair in the first register
```
MOVDQA XMM1, XMMWORD PTR [ nums1 ]
MINPS XMM1, XMM2
```

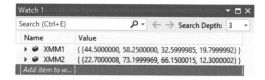
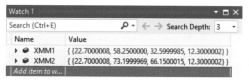

5 Finally, add statements to round all values, then place the average of each pair in the first register
```
ROUNDPS XMM1, XMM1, 00b
ROUNDPS XMM2, XMM2, 00b
PAVGW XMM1, XMM2
```

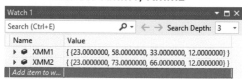

6 Set a breakpoint, then run the code and click **Step Into**

7 Examine the Watch window to see maximum, minimum, rounded, and average values of each pair

Managing Vectors

Advanced Vector Extensions (AVX) provide two major advantages over Streaming SIMD Extensions (SSE):

- AVX registers (**YMM0-YMM15**) are 256 bits wide, so can operate simultaneously on eight **REAL4** 32-bit single-precision, or four **REAL8** 64-bit double-precision pieces of data.

- AVX instructions take three operands, assigning the result of an operation on two operands to a third operand. For this reason, AVX instructions are said to be "non-destructive".

AVX regards arrays as "vectors" and has similar instruction names to those in SSE, but prefixed with a letter **V** (for vector). For example, the equivalent of the SSE **MOVAPS** instruction (move, aligned, packed, single precision) becomes **VMOVAPS** (vector, move, aligned, packed, single precision) in AVX.

For AVX instructions, a **YMMWORD** data type represents 256 bits. This can be used with a **PTR** (pointer) directive to assign 256 bits of data to a **YMM** register. The operation has this syntax:

> **VMOVPS** *Register-Name* , **YMMWORD PTR** [*Source*]

There are several AVX instructions to perform simultaneous arithmetical operations on multiple values for both single-precision and double-precision floating-point numbers:

Instruction	
VADDPS *Register-Name* , *Register-Name, Register/Variable*	Add
VADDPD *Register-Name* , *Register-Name, Register/Variable*	
VSUBPS *Register-Name* , *Register-Name, Register/Variable*	Subtract
VSUBPD *Register-Name* , *Register-Name, Register/Variable*	
VMULPS *Register-Name* , *Register-Name, Register/Variable*	Multiply
VMULPD *Register-Name* , *Register-Name, Register/Variable*	
VDIVPS *Register-Name* , *Register-Name, Register/Variable*	Divide
VDIVPD *Register-Name* , *Register-Name, Register/Variable*	

In each case, the arithmetical instructions place the result of the operation in the first operand – preserving the original values in the second and third operands.

Arrays are indexed structures of a fixed size, whereas vectors are non-indexed structures that can be resized.

146

AVX instructions are non-destructive.

1 Create a new project named "AVX" from the **MASM Template**, then open the **Source.asm** file

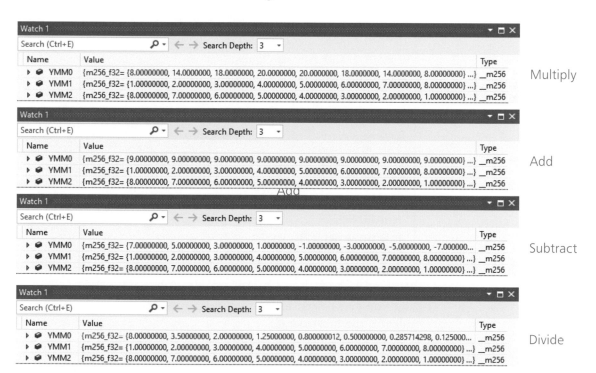

ASM

AVX

2 In the **.DATA** section of the file, initialize two vectors
vec1 REAL4 1.0, 2.0, 3.0, 4.0, 5.0, 6.0, 7.0, 8.0
vec2 REAL4 8.0, 7.0, 6.0, 5.0, 4.0, 3.0, 2.0, 1.0

3 Next, in the **.CODE main** procedure, add statements to assign the vectors to registers
VMOVAPS YMM1, YMMWORD PTR [vec1]
VMOVAPS YMM2, YMMWORD PTR [vec2]

4 Add statements to perform arithmetical operations on each pair of elements, placing the result in a third register
VMULPS YMM0, YMM1, YMM2
VADDPS YMM0, YMM1, YMM2
VSUBPS YMM0, YMM2, YMM1
VDIVPS YMM0, YMM2, YMM1

5 Set a breakpoint, then run the code and click **Step Into** to see the results in the **YMM0** register

Watch 1			
Search (Ctrl+E)	🔎 ▾ ← → Search Depth: 3 ▾		
Name	Value		Type
▶ ● YMM0	{m256_f32= {8.00000000, 14.0000000, 18.0000000, 20.0000000, 20.0000000, 18.0000000, 14.0000000, 8.00000000} ...}		_m256
▶ ● YMM1	{m256_f32= {1.00000000, 2.00000000, 3.00000000, 4.00000000, 5.00000000, 6.00000000, 7.00000000, 8.00000000} ...}		_m256
▶ ● YMM2	{m256_f32= {8.00000000, 7.00000000, 6.00000000, 5.00000000, 4.00000000, 3.00000000, 2.00000000, 1.00000000} ...}		_m256

Multiply

Watch 1			
Search (Ctrl+E)	🔎 ▾ ← → Search Depth: 3 ▾		
Name	Value		Type
▶ ● YMM0	{m256_f32= {9.00000000, 9.00000000, 9.00000000, 9.00000000, 9.00000000, 9.00000000, 9.00000000, 9.00000000} ...}		_m256
▶ ● YMM1	{m256_f32= {1.00000000, 2.00000000, 3.00000000, 4.00000000, 5.00000000, 6.00000000, 7.00000000, 8.00000000} ...}		_m256
▶ ● YMM2	{m256_f32= {8.00000000, 7.00000000, 6.00000000, 5.00000000, 4.00000000, 3.00000000, 2.00000000, 1.00000000} ...}		_m256

Add

Watch 1			
Search (Ctrl+E)	🔎 ▾ ← → Search Depth: 3 ▾		
Name	Value		Type
▶ ● YMM0	{m256_f32= {7.00000000, 5.00000000, 3.00000000, 1.00000000, -1.00000000, -3.00000000, -5.00000000, -7.000000...		_m256
▶ ● YMM1	{m256_f32= {1.00000000, 2.00000000, 3.00000000, 4.00000000, 5.00000000, 6.00000000, 7.00000000, 8.00000000} ...}		_m256
▶ ● YMM2	{m256_f32= {8.00000000, 7.00000000, 6.00000000, 5.00000000, 4.00000000, 3.00000000, 2.00000000, 1.00000000} ...}		_m256

Subtract

Watch 1			
Search (Ctrl+E)	🔎 ▾ ← → Search Depth: 3 ▾		
Name	Value		Type
▶ ● YMM0	{m256_f32= {8.00000000, 3.50000000, 2.00000000, 1.25000000, 0.800000012, 0.500000000, 0.285714298, 0.125000...		_m256
▶ ● YMM1	{m256_f32= {1.00000000, 2.00000000, 3.00000000, 4.00000000, 5.00000000, 6.00000000, 7.00000000, 8.00000000} ...}		_m256
▶ ● YMM2	{m256_f32= {8.00000000, 7.00000000, 6.00000000, 5.00000000, 4.00000000, 3.00000000, 2.00000000, 1.00000000} ...}		_m256

Divide

Fusing Operations

The Advanced Vector Extensions (AVX) have a further instruction set to perform Fused Multiply Add (FMA) operations on scalars, and vectors. These provide improved performance by computing both multiplication and addition in a single CPU clock cycle, rather than the two clock cycles needed for separate multiplication and addition instructions.

The FMA instructions take three operands and include a three-figure numerical pattern. For example, the scalar single-precision FMA instruction has this syntax:

VFMADD*xxx***SS** *Register-Name* , *Register-Name, Register/Variable*

The numerical pattern within an FMA instruction represents the first operand with a 1, the second with a 2, and the third with a 3. This pattern determines the order of the operation. The first two numbers are the operands that will be multiplied, and the third number is the operand that will finally be added to the result.

The FMA instructions can be used with the SSE **XMM** registers or with the AVX **YMM** registers. The various instructions are listed in the table below, together with their order of operation:

Instruction	Data Type	Operation Order
VFMADD132SS	Scalar Single Precision	
VFMADD132SD	Scalar Double Precision	1st x 3rd, + 2nd operand
VFMADD132PS	Packed Single Precision	
VFMADD132PD	Packed Double Precision	
VFMADD213SS	Scalar Single Precision	
VFMADD213SD	Scalar Double Precision	2nd x 1st, + 3rd operand
VFMADD213PS	Packed Single Precision	
VFMADD213PD	Packed Double Precision	
VFMADD231SS	Scalar Single Precision	
VFMADD231SD	Scalar Double Precision	2nd x 3rd, + 1st operand
VFMADD231PS	Packed Single Precision	
VFMADD231PD	Packed Double Precision	

With all FMA instructions, the result of the multiplication and addition gets placed in the first operand – destroying the original value in the first operand.

Don't forget

You can only use the numerical combinations listed here. Other combinations, such as **VFMADD123SS**, produce a syntax error.

...cont'd

1 Create a new project named "FMA" from the **MASM Template**, then open the **Source.asm** file

ASM

FMA

2 In the **.DATA** section of the file, initialize three scalars
numA REAL4 2.0
numB REAL4 8.0
numC REAL4 5.0

3 Next, in the **.CODE main** procedure, add statements to assign the scalars to registers
MOVSS XMM0, numA
MOVSS XMM1, numB
MOVSS XMM2, numC

4 Now, add statements to multiply and add the scalar values in three different combinations
VFMADD132SS XMM0, XMM1, XMM2   *; 1st x 3rd + 2nd*
MOVSS XMM0, numA
VFMADD213SS XMM0, XMM1, XMM2   *; 2nd x 1st + 3rd*
MOVSS XMM0, numA
VFMADD231SS XMM0, XMM1, XMM2   *; 2nd x 3rd + 1st*

5 Set a breakpoint, then run the code and click **Step Into** to see the results in the first register

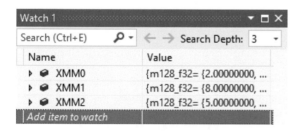

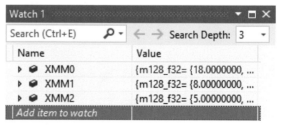

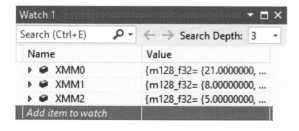

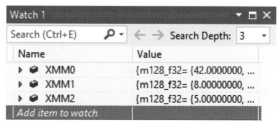

Summary

- Streaming SIMD Extensions (SSE) added 128-bit **XMM** CPU registers for simultaneous floating-point arithmetic.

- Advanced Vector Extensions (AVX) added 256-bit **YMM** CPU registers for simultaneous floating-point arithmetic.

- SSE and AVX can pack arithmetical instructions into fixed same-size lanes for simultaneous floating-point arithmetic.

- For SSE, an **XMMWORD** data type represents 128 bits, and for AVX, a **YMMWORD** data type represents 256 bits.

- The **PTR** directive can be used to assign **XMMWORD** values to **XMM** registers, or **YMMWORD** values to **YMM** registers.

- SSE and AVX instructions are mnemonics that describe the operation and the type of data for that operation.

- SSE requires its data to be aligned to 16-byte boundaries, and this may be achieved using an **ALIGN 16** instruction.

- In both single-precision 32-bit format and double-precision 64-bit format, the MSB indicates the sign of the number.

- The **REAL4** data type is 32-bit and the **REAL8** is 64-bit.

- Floating-point numbers can be assigned to **XMM** registers using **MOVAPS**, **MOVAPD**, **MOVSS** or **MOVSD** instructions.

- SSE instructions **ADDPS**, **SUBPS**, **MULPS**, and **DIVPS** perform arithmetic on packed single-precision floating-point numbers.

- Saturation arithmetic limits operations to a fixed range, and can be used to indicate problems with integer arithmetic.

- The specialized instructions **MINPS**, **MAXPS**, **ROUNDPS** and **PAVGB** perform useful calculations.

- SSE instructions take two operands and are destructive; AVX instructions take three operands and are non-destructive.

- AVX has similar instruction names to those in SSE, but prefixed with a letter **V** – so **MOVAPS** becomes **VMOVAPS**.

- FMA instructions take three operands and include a numerical pattern that determines the operation order.

10 Calling Windows

Calling Convention

A calling convention is a set of rules that specify how arguments may be passed from the caller, to which register they must be assigned, which registers must be preserved, in which register the return value will be placed, and who must balance the stack.

If you want to call a Windows function in the **kernel32.lib** library, you need to know its calling convention to be sure of the effect.

Microsoft x64 Calling Convention

For x64 programming on Windows, the x64 Application Binary Interface (ABI) uses a four-register "fast-call" calling convention, with these requirements:

- The first four arguments passed to, or returned from, a function are placed in specific registers. For integers: the first in **RCX**; the second in **RDX**; the third in **R8**; and the fourth in **R9**. For floating-point values: the first in **XMM0**; the second in **XMM1**; the third in **XMM2**; and the fourth in **XMM3**.

- The registers for arguments, plus **RAX, R10, R11, XMM4** and **XMM5** are considered volatile – so, if used, their values should be preserved before calling other procedures.

- If the function call receives more than four arguments, the additional arguments will be placed sequentially on the stack.

- The return value will be placed in the **RAX** register.

- Before making a function call, the **RSP** register must be aligned on a 16-byte boundary, where its memory address is exactly divisible by 16.

- Before making a function call, "shadow space" must be provided on the stack to reserve space for four arguments – even if the function passes fewer than four arguments. Typically, this is 32 bytes, but may need to be greater when calling a Windows function that returns more arguments.

- It is the caller's responsibility to clean up the stack.

- The caller must finally remove the shadow space allocated for arguments and any return values.

To interact with the Windows console from an x64 Assembly program, you first need grab a standard "device handle" using the **GetStdHandle** function in the **kernel32.lib** library.

GetStdHandle Function

This function requires a single **DWORD** device code argument to specify a device type, which can be one of the following:

Name	Device Code	Device Type
STD_INPUT_HANDLE	-10	Console input buffer
STD_OUTPUT_HANDLE	-11	Active console screen
STD_ERROR_HANDLE	-12	Active console screen

This function returns the appropriate device handle to the **RAX** register, which can be saved in a variable for later use.

A program can then write output in the Windows console by calling the **WriteConsoleA** function in the **kernel32.lib** library.

WriteConsoleA Function

This function accepts these four arguments:

● The device output handle acquired by **GetStdHandle**.

● A pointer to an array of the characters to be written, specified as a null-terminated string (ending with a zero character).

● The total number of characters to be written.

● Optionally, a pointer to a variable to receive the number of characters actually written.

In x64 programming, all pointers are 64 bits wide.

When a call to the **WriteConsoleA** function has been successful, the function returns a non-zero value (**1**) to the **RAX** register, but if the call fails, it returns a zero (**0**) to the **RAX** register.

The example on pages 154-155 will first call the **GetStdHandle** function to acquire the console's **STD_OUTPUT_HANDLE**, then call the **WriteConsoleA** function to write output in a console window.

Writing Output

HELLO

An Assembly program can employ the Microsoft x64 Calling Convention to write a traditional message in a console window, using the **GetStdHandle** and **WriteConsoleA** functions described on page 153. For console programs, it is necessary to configure the linker to use the Console SubSystem in the program's properties.

1 Create a new project named "HELLO" from the **MASM Template**, then open the **Source.asm** file

2 On the Visual Studio toolbar, click **Debug**, **Properties**, **Linker**, **System** and change the **SubSystem** to **Console(/SUBSYSTEM:CONSOLE)** – then click **Apply**, **OK**

3 Just below the **ExitProcess PROTO** directive, add further directives to import two more library functions plus a constant containing the output device code
GetStdHandle PROTO
WriteConsoleA PROTO
deviceCode EQU -11

4 In the **.DATA** section of the file, initialize a character array as a null-terminated string, plus variables to store a handle and the number of characters written
txt BYTE 10, " Hello World! ", 10, 10, 0
handle QWORD ?
num BYTE ?

Hot tip

The number **10** included in the character array is the ASCII line feed character code, and is included merely to format the output.

5 Now, in the **.CODE main** procedure, add statements to zero the five registers to be used in this program – adhering to the Microsoft x64 Calling Convention
XOR RAX, RAX
XOR RCX, RCX
XOR RDX, RDX
XOR R8, R8
XOR R9, R9

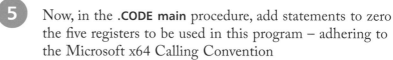

Watch 1		▾ ₄ ×
Search (Ctrl+E)	🔎 ▾ ← → Search Depth:	3 ▾
Name	Value	
🔵 RAX,X	0x0000000000000000	
🔵 RCX,X	0x0000000000000000	
🔵 RDX,X	0x0000000000000000	
🔵 R8	0	
🔵 R9,X	0x0000000000000000	
🔒 num	0	
Add item to watch		

6 Add a statement to allocate shadow space for arguments
SUB RSP, 32

7 Next, add statements to acquire the console's **STD_OUTPUT_HANDLE** and store it in a variable

```
MOV RCX, deviceCode    ; Pass device code as argument 1.
CALL GetStdHandle
MOV handle, RAX                ; Store the device handle.
```

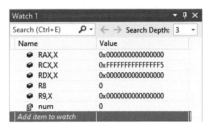 

Returned device handle.

8 Pass the arguments required to write to the console, and remember to rebalance the stack

```
MOV RCX, handle        ; Pass device handle as arg1.
LEA RDX, txt           ; Pass pointer to array as arg2.
MOV R8, LENGTHOF txt   ; Pass array length as arg3.
LEA R9, num            ; Pass pointer to variable as arg4.
CALL WriteConsoleA
ADD RSP, 32
```

Returned success status.

Returned number of characters written.

9 Set a breakpoint, then run the code and examine the Watch window to see the arguments and returned values

10 On the Visual Studio toolbar, click **Debug, Start Without Debugging** to see the console message output

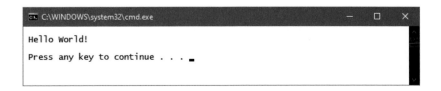

Reading Input

A program can read input from the Windows console by calling the **ReadConsoleA** function in the **kernel32.lib** library.

ReadConsoleA Function

This function accepts these four arguments:

● The device input handle acquired by **GetStdHandle**.

● A pointer to an array in which to store the characters read.

● The total number of characters to be read.

● A pointer to a variable to receive the number of characters actually read.

When a call to the **ReadConsoleA** function has been successful, the function returns a non-zero value (**1**) to the **RAX** register, but if the call fails, it returns a zero (**0**) to the **RAX** register.

The Assembly code for reading console input is very similar to that for writing to the console, described in the previous example.

1 Create a new project named "ENTER" from the **MASM Template**, then open the **Source.asm** file

2 On the Visual Studio toolbar, click **Debug**, **Properties**, **Linker**, **System** and change the **SubSystem** to **Console(/SUBSYSTEM:CONSOLE)** – then click **Apply**, **OK**

3 Copy Steps 3-8 from the previous example – to be edited so this program will read instead of write

4 Change the statement that imports the writing function to import the reading function
ReadConsoleA PROTO

5 Change the constant's value from **-11** to now acquire the console's **STD_INPUT_HANDLE**
deviceCode EQU -10

6 In the **.DATA** section of the file, change the character array to become a longer, but empty, array
txt BYTE 100 DUP (?)

ASM

ENTER

Hot tip

You can copy and paste the previous **Source.asm** content into Notepad, then start a new project and copy and paste from Notepad into the new **Source.asm** file.

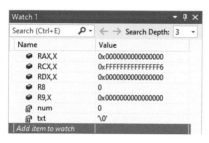

...cont'd

7 Now, in the **.CODE main** procedure, change the call from **WriteConsoleA** so the program will now read input
CALL ReadConsoleA

8 Set a breakpoint, then run the code and examine the Watch window to see the arguments and returned values

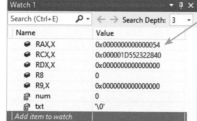

Returned device handle.

9 See a console window appear when the program calls the **ReadConsoleA** function

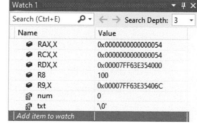

10 Type some text at the prompt in the console window, then hit the **Enter** key to see your text get read into the array

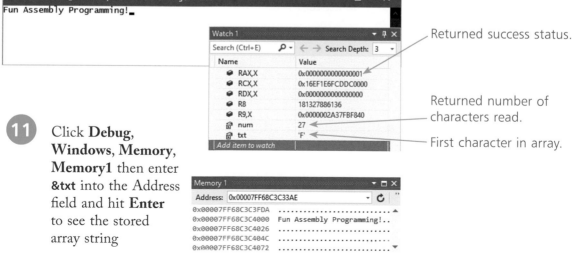

Returned success status.

Returned number of characters read.

First character in array.

11 Click **Debug, Windows, Memory, Memory1** then enter **&txt** into the Address field and hit **Enter** to see the stored array string

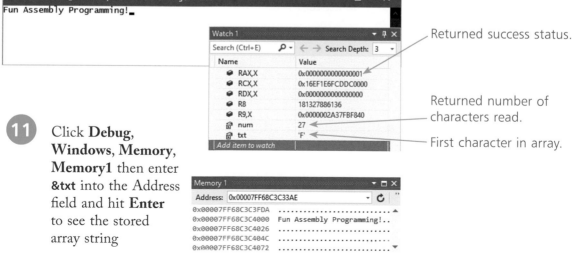

157

Grabbing File Handles

In order to work with files, an Assembly program first needs to acquire a handle to that file. The Windows ABI function for this purpose is the **CreateFileA** function, which can not only create a new file but also open an existing file for operations.

CreateFileA Function

This function accepts seven arguments and returns a file handle:

- A pointer to a string specifying the file's name and path.

- The desired access mode specified using a "bit mask", in which specific bits can represent any of these access rights:

GENERIC_READ	080000000h	Read a file
GENERIC_WRITE	040000000h	Write a file
GENERIC_EXECUTE	020000000h	Execute a file
GENERIC_ALL	010000000h	Read, Write, Execute

- The desired sharing mode specified using a bit mask, in which specific bits can represent either of these sharing rights:

FILE_SHARE_READ	1	Share reading
FILE_SHARE_WRITE	2	Share writing

- The desired security mode, which can be **NULL** (0) to use a default security descriptor that prevents the handle from being used by any child processes the program may create.

- The desired creation mode specified using a constant value, in which specific bits can represent any of these rights:

CREATE_NEW	1	New file if none exists
CREATE_ALWAYS	2	New or overwrites existing file
OPEN_EXISTING	3	Open only if existing
OPEN_ALWAYS	4	Open existing or create new file

- The desired file attributes specified using a mask, in which specific bits can typically represent this right:

FILE_ATTRIBUTE_NORMAL	128	No restrictive attributes

- A handle to a template file specifying file attributes, which can be **NULL** (0) and is ignored when opening an existing file.

Hot tip

A file handle is a temporary reference number that the operating system assigns to a file requested by a program. The system interacts with the file via its temporary reference number until the program closes the file or the program ends.

...cont'd

Rather than assigning the arguments to the **CreateFileA** function parameters as numerical values, it is preferable to assign the values to their names so that constant names can be used to make the program code more readable.

Adhering to the Microsoft x64 Calling Convention, an Assembly program must typically provide 32 bytes of shadow space on the stack to reserve space for four arguments. This means that the stack pointer moves down to a lower memory location:

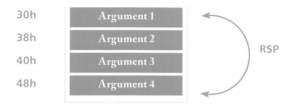

As the **CreateFileA** function requires seven arguments, the program must also assign three further arguments to the stack. The stack pointer is now moved, so the extra three arguments can be assigned to memory locations using offsets to the current stack pointer to contain quad word sized values.

30h	Argument 1	RSP
38h	Argument 2	
40h	Argument 3	
48h	Argument 4	
50h	Argument 5	RSP+32
58h	Argument 6	RSP+40
60h	Argument 7	RSP+48
68h	Argument 8	RSP+56

The **QWORD** data type, representing 64 bits, can be used with a **PTR** (pointer) directive to assign each of the three additional arguments to the offset memory locations, using this syntax:

```
MOV QWORD PTR [ Memory-Address ] , Argument-Value
```

Creating Files

As described on page 159, an Assembly program can create a file, or open an existing file, by calling the **CreateFileA** function in the **kernel32.lib** library.

This example will be enlarged in ensuing examples to demonstrate writing to files by calling a **WriteFile** function, and reading from files by calling a **ReadFile** function:

1 Create a new project named "CREATE" from the **MASM Template**, then open the **Source.asm** file

2 Just below the **ExitProcess PROTO** directive, add a further directive to import another library function
CreateFileA PROTO

3 Below the added import directive, define constants for file access mask values
GENERIC_READ	**EQU 080000000h**
GENERIC_WRITE	**EQU 040000000h**
FILE_SHARE_READ	**EQU 1**
FILE_SHARE_WRITE	**EQU 2**
OPEN_ALWAYS	**EQU 4**
FILE_ATTRIBUTE_NORMAL	**EQU 128**

Don't forget

Replace the *username* placeholder in Step 4 with your own username on your PC.

4 In the **.DATA** section of the file, initialize a character array with a path and file name for a new file and declare a variable to store a file handle
filePath BYTE "C:/Users/username**/Desktop/Quote.txt"**
fileHandle QWORD ?

5 In the **.CODE main** procedure, add statements to zero the five registers to be used in this program – adhering to the Microsoft x64 Calling Convention
XOR RAX, RAX
XOR RCX, RCX
XOR RDX, RDX
XOR R8, R8
XOR R9, R9

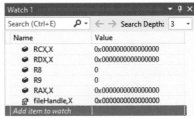

6 Add a statement to allocate shadow space for arguments
SUB RSP, 64

7 Next, add statements to pass arguments via shadow space
```
LEA RCX, filePath
MOV RDX, GENERIC_READ OR GENERIC_WRITE
MOV R8, FILE_SHARE_READ OR FILE_SHARE_WRITE
MOV R9, 0
```

8 Now, add statements to pass additional arguments via stack offsets
```
MOV QWORD PTR [ RSP+32 ], OPEN_ALWAYS
MOV QWORD PTR [ RSP+40 ], FILE_ATTRIBUTE_NORMAL
MOV QWORD PTR [ RSP+48 ], 0
```

9 Then, call the function to pass the arguments to its parameters and create a file
```
CALL CreateFileA
```

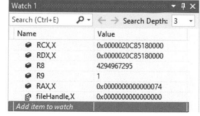

10 Add an instruction to save the file handle in a variable – for further use in two ensuing examples
```
MOV fileHandle, RAX
```

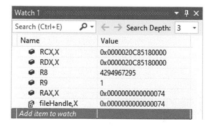

11 Finally, remember to rebalance the stack
```
ADD RSP, 64
```

12 Set a breakpoint, then run the code and examine the Watch window to see the arguments and returned file handle – and see the new file icon on your desktop

Writing Files

A program can write to a file by grabbing its file handle, then calling the **WriteFile** function in the **kernel32.lib** library.

WriteFile Function

This function accepts these five arguments:

- The file handle acquired by **CreateFileA**.

- A pointer to an array of the characters to be written.

- The total number of characters to be written.

- A pointer to a variable to receive the number of bytes written.

- A pointer to an "overlapped structure", which can be **NULL** (0).

When a call to the **WriteFile** function succeeds, it returns a non-zero value (**1**) to the **RAX** register, or if it fails, it returns a zero (**0**).

WRITER

1 Create a new project named "WRITER" from the **MASM Template**, then open the **Source.asm** file

2 Copy all code from the CREATE example, described on pages 160-161, into your new project

3 Just below the **ExitProcess PROTO** directive, add a directive to import another library function
WriteFile PROTO

4 Below the added import directive, create a macro to zero the five registers to be used in this program
clearRegisters MACRO
XOR RAX, RAX
XOR RCX, RCX
XOR RDX, RDX
XOR R8, R8
XOR R9, R9
ENDM

An overlapped structure can be used to specify positions within the file at which to start and finish reading.

5 In the .**DATA** section of the file, initialize a character array with a string to be written into a file, and a variable to receive the number of bytes written
txt BYTE "The truth is rarely pure and never simple."
num DWORD ?

6 At the start of the **.CODE main** procedure, replace the individual zeroing instructions with a call to the macro **clearRegisters**

7 Immediately below the **MOV fileHandle, RAX** instruction that saves the file handle, call the macro again and add instructions to pass arguments via shadow space
clearRegisters
MOV RCX, fileHandle
LEA RDX, txt
MOV R8, LENGTHOF txt
LEA R9, num

8 Now, add an instruction to pass one additional argument via a stack offset
MOV QWORD PTR [RSP+32], 0

9 Then, call the function to pass the arguments to its parameters and write into a file
CALL WriteFile

10 Set a breakpoint, then run the code and examine the Watch window to see the arguments passed

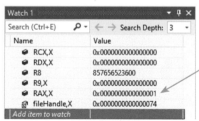

Returned success status.

11 Open the file in a text editor to confirm that the text has indeed been written into the file

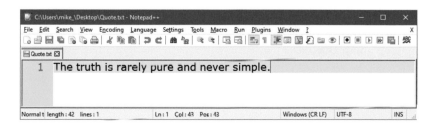

Reading Files

A program can read from a file by grabbing its file handle then calling the **ReadFile** function in the **kernel32.lib** library.

ReadFile Function

This function accepts these five arguments:

● The file handle acquired by **CreateFileA**.

● A pointer to an array where read characters will be saved.

● The total number of bytes to read.

● A pointer to a variable to receive the number of bytes read.

● A pointer to a quad word "overlapped structure", or **NULL** (0).

When a call to the **ReadFile** function succeeds, it returns a non-zero value (**1**) to the **RAX** register, or if it fails, it returns a zero (**0**).

READER

1 Create a new project named "READER" from the **MASM Template**, then open the **Source.asm** file

2 On the Visual Studio toolbar, click **Debug**, **Properties**, **Linker**, **System** and change the **SubSystem** to **Console(/SUBSYSTEM:CONSOLE)** – then click **Apply**, **OK**

3 Copy all code from the WRITER example, described on pages 162-163, into your new project

4 Just below the **ExitProcess PROTO** directive, add directives to import three more library functions
ReadFile PROTO
GetStdHandle PROTO
WriteConsoleA PROTO

Copy the previous **Source.asm** content, then start a new project and directly paste into the new **Source.asm** file.

5 In the **.DATA** section of the file, initialize an empty array with a capacity of 100 bytes (characters), and a variable to receive the number of bytes read
buffer BYTE 100 DUP (?)
num DWORD ?

6 After the second macro, call in the **.CODE main** procedure, change **txt** to **buffer**, and call from **WriteFile** to **ReadFile**

```
LEA RCX, fileHandle
MOV RDX, buffer
MOV R8, LENGTHOF buffer
LEA R9, num
MOV QWORD PTR [ RSP+32 ], 0
CALL ReadFile
```

7 Set a breakpoint, then run the code and examine the Watch window to see the file read successfully

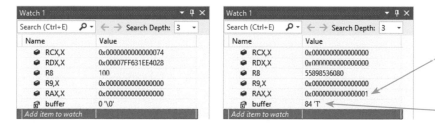

— Returned success status.

— First read character.

8 To write the read file's contents to the console, first add instructions to acquire the console's **STD_OUTPUT_HANDLE** immediately after the call to the **ReadFile** function

```
MOV RCX, -11          ; Pass device code as argument 1.
CALL GetStdHandle     ; Return handle to RAX.
```

9 Pass the arguments required to write to the console, then call the **WriteConsoleA** function

```
MOV RCX, RAX
LEA RDX, buffer
MOV R8, LENGTHOF buffer
CALL WriteConsoleA
```

10 On the Visual Studio menu bar, click **Debug, Start Without Debugging** to see the buffer content output

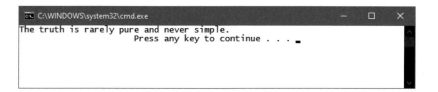

Opening Dialogs

A program can open a Windows message box dialog by calling the **MessageBoxA** function in the **user32.lib** library.

MessageBoxA Function

This function accepts these four arguments:

- The handle to the owner window of the message box, or **NULL** (0) if the message box has no owner window.

- A pointer to an array that is a message string.

- A pointer to an array that is the message box title.

- A combination of flags specifying the dialog type and icon as the total sum of one type value plus one icon value. Listed below are some of the possible values:

MB_OK (the default)	0
MB_OKCANCEL	1
MB_ABORTRETRYIGNORE	2
MB_YESNOCANCEL	3
MB_CANCELTRYCONTINUE	6
MB_ICONERROR	16
MB_ICONQUESTION	32
MB_ICONWARNING	48
MB_ICONINFORMATION	64

When a call to the **MessageBoxA** function fails, it returns zero, but if it succeeds, it returns one of these values to the **RAX** register, indicating which button the user selected:

IDOK (the default)	1
IDCANCEL	2
IDABORT	3
IDRETRY	4
IDIGNORE	5
IDYES	6
IDNO	7
IDTRYAGAIN	10
IDCONTINUE	11

① Create a new project named "MSGBOX" from the **MASM Template**, then open the **Source.asm** file

MSGBOX

② At the start of the program, add directives to import a library containing Windows' desktop functions and import one of those functions
INCLUDELIB user32.lib
MessageBoxA PROTO

③ In the **.DATA** section of the file, initialize two variables with message and title null-terminated strings
msg BYTE "Are you ready to continue...", 0
ttl BYTE "Assembly x64 Programming", 0

④ In the **.CODE main** procedure, clear a register and align the stack, then allocate shadow space for four arguments
XOR RAX, RAX
AND RSP, -16   ; *Align the stack to 16 bytes.*
SUB RSP, 32   ; *Shadow space for 4 x 8 bytes.*

Don't forget

The Microsoft x64 Calling Convention requires the stack to be 16-byte aligned. When this program starts, that is not the case, so the **AND** instruction is used here to move the stack pointer down to the next 16-byte aligned address.

⑤ Now, add the arguments required to create a dialog, then call the **MessageBoxA** function
MOV RCX, 0   ; *Pass no owner window as arg1.*
LEA RDX, msg   ; *Pass pointer to array as arg2.*
LEA R8, ttl   ; *Pass pointer to array as arg3.*
MOV R9, 35   ; *Pass combined type as arg4.*
CALL MessageBoxA   ; *Receive returned value.*

⑥ Rebalance the stack
ADD RSP, 32   ; *Rebalance for four arguments.*

⑦ Set a breakpoint, then run the code and click **Step Into**

⑧ Click the **Yes** button when the dialog box appears, then examine the Watch window to see the returned values

Returned button value.

Summary

- The Microsoft x64 Calling Convention uses registers **RCX**, **RDX**, **R8** and **R9** to pass arguments to function parameters, and requires the **RSP** register to be aligned on a 16-byte boundary.

- Floating-point values can be passed to functions using the **XMM0**, **XMM1**, **XMM2** and **XMM3** registers.

- If a function call receives more than four arguments, the additional arguments will be placed on the stack, and each argument pushed onto the stack is 64 bits in size.

- Before calling a function, the program must typically reserve 32 bytes of shadow space for four arguments.

- The linker must be configured to use the Console SubSystem in order to interact with the Windows console.

- The **GetStdHandle** function in the **kernel32.lib** library can return a device handle for interaction with the console.

- The **WriteConsoleA** function sends output to a console screen.

- The **ReadConsoleA** function reads input from a console screen.

- The **CreateFileA** function can create a new file, or open an existing file, and it returns a file handle.

- The file access values required by the **CreateFileA** function can be assigned to constants for better readability.

- When a function requires more than four arguments, the additional arguments can be assigned to memory locations using offsets to the current stack pointer.

- The **WriteFile** function writes text into a file, using the file handle returned by the **CreateFileA** function.

- The **ReadFile** function reads text from a file, using the file handle returned by the **CreateFileA** function.

- The **user32.lib** library contains Windows' desktop functions.

- The **MessageBoxA** function creates dialog boxes containing various combinations of text, icons, and buttons.

- The value returned by the **MessageBoxA** function indicates which dialog button was selected by the user.

11 Incorporating Code

Splitting Code

As the size of Assembly programs grow longer, it is often preferable to separate the code into individual files to make the code more manageable. Additionally, the modularization of similar functionality is useful to reuse particular files in other projects.

The simplest way to split the code is to create an additional **.asm** file in the project and move all procedures except the **main** procedure into the new file.

SPLIT
MathF.asm

1 Create a new project named "SPLIT" from the **MASM Template**

2 In the Solution Explorer window, right-click on the project name, then choose **Add**, **New Item**

3 Select a C++ file and rename it **MathF.asm**, then click **Add**

4 Open **MathF.asm** in the Editor window, then add a **.CODE** section containing four simple arithmetic functions

```
.CODE
DoAdd PROC
MOV RAX, RCX
ADD RAX, RDX
RET
DoAdd ENDP

DoSub PROC
MOV RAX, RCX
SUB RAX, RDX
RET
DoSub ENDP

DoMul PROC
MUL RCX
RET
DoMul ENDP

DoDiv PROC
SHR RAX, 1
DIV RCX
RET
DoDiv ENDP
END
```

The external file doesn't need its own **INCLUDELIB** directive, as the **kernel32.lib** library is imported by the directive in the main file.

5 Next, open the **Source.asm** file and define the external symbols, just below the **ExitProcess PROTO** directive
DoAdd PROTO
DoSub PROTO
DoMul PROTO
DoDiv PROTO

SPLIT
Source.asm

6 Now, in the **.CODE main** procedure, add instructions to call each external function
MOV RCX, 8
MOV RDX, 16
CALL DoAdd

MOV RCX, 9
MOV RDX, 3
CALL DoSub

CALL DoMul
CALL DoDiv

7 Set a breakpoint, then run the code and examine the Watch window to see the values modified by external functions – just as if they were written in the **main** program file

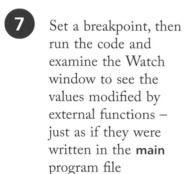

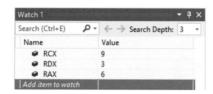

Click the [Step Into] **Step Into** button to step through each line in both files,

or click the [Step] **Step Over** button to step only through each line in the **main** procedure.

8 Notice that the **DoDiv** function uses a **SHR** instruction to first divide by two, then divides by the value nine in **RCX**

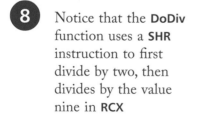

Making Code Libraries

An alternative to splitting code into individual .asm files, demonstrated in the previous example, is to create a library file that references external procedures. This can be added to the **main** program file with an **INCLUDELIB** directive, and individual functions imported with the **PROTO** directive as usual.

The technique to create a library file first requires the assembler to create **.obj** object files for each external file that is to be included in the library. These can then be specified to the command-line Microsoft Library Manager (**lib.exe**), which will generate the **.lib** library file that can be included in the **main** program file.

LIB

1 Create a new project named "LIB" from the **MASM Template**

2 In the Solution Explorer window, right-click on the project name, then choose **Add**, **New Item**

3 Add a **MathF.asm** file and copy in the code from **MathF.asm** in the previous SPLIT example

4 With **MathF.asm** open in the Editor window, select **x64** on the toolbar and click **Build**, **Compile** to create an object file – this will be placed in the project's **x64\Debug** folder

The Library Manager requires an object file to be created for each Assembly **.asm** file to be included in a library.

5 Next, on the menu bar, select **Tools**, **Command Line**, **Developer Command Prompt** to open a console window

6 Enter this command to locate the prompt in the folder containing the newly-created object file
CD x64\Debug

7 Then, enter this command to create a library file from the newly-created object file
LIB /OUT:MathF.lib /verbose MathF.obj

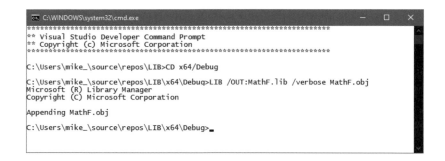

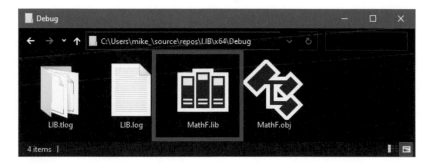

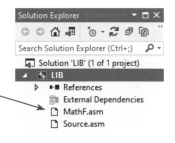

8 In the Solution Explorer window, right-click on the **MathF.asm** file icon, then choose **Remove, Delete** to delete the file from this project

9 Open the **Source.asm** file in the Editor window, and copy in the code from **Source.asm in** the previous example

10 Finally, insert a line just below the **ExitProcess PROTO** directive, to locate the newly-created library file (inserting your own username in the path)
INCLUDELIB C:\Users\mike_\source\repos\LIB\x64\Debug\MathF.lib

11 Set a breakpoint, then run the code and examine the Watch window to see the program run as before

Calling Assembly Code

To combine the convenience and abilities of a high-level language with the speed of performance provided by directly addressing the CPU registers, Assembly code functions can be called from within a high-level program. This is achieved in C++ (and C) programming simply by adding definitions of the Assembly functions within the high-level language code.

An Assembly function definition in C++ begins with the **extern** keyword followed by **"C"** (must be uppercase), then the function signature specifying return data type, name, parameter/s data type.

Arguments are passed to the **RCX**, **RDX**, **R8** and **R9** registers, as with the Microsoft x64 Calling Convention.

CALL
Source.asm

1 Create a new C++ **Console App** project named "CALL"

2 In the Solution Explorer window, right-click on the project name, then choose **Build Dependencies**, **Build Customizations** – to open a "Visual C++ Build Customization Files" dialog

3 In the dialog, check the **masm(.targets, .props)** item, then click the **OK** button to close the dialog

4 In Solution Explorer, right-click on the project CALL icon, then choose **Add, New Item**

5 Select **C++ File**, then change its name to **Source.asm** and click **ADD** to add the file to the project

6 Open **Source.asm** in the Editor window, then add a **.CODE** section containing a function to simply add two received arguments and return their sum total

```
.CODE

DoSum PROC
MOV RAX, RCX
ADD RAX, RDX
RET
DoSum ENDP

END
```

...cont'd

7 Next, open **CALL.cpp** in the Editor window, and delete all its default content

CALL
CALL.cpp

8 Add the standard C++ inclusions and a definition of the external Assembly function

```
#include <iostream>
using namespace std;

extern "C" int DoSum(int, int);
```

9 Now, add the main C++ program function that requests two numbers and passes them to the Assembly function

```
int main( ) {
  int num, plus = 0;
  cout << "Enter Number: ";     cin >> num;
  cout << "Enter Another: ";    cin >> plus;
  cout << "Total: " << DoSum(num, plus) << endl;
  return 0;
}
```

Explanation of the C++ code is outside the remit of this book, but you can refer to the companion book in this series entitled **C++ Programming in easy steps** to learn about that programming language.

10 On the Visual Studio menu bar, change the build configuration to **x64**

11 On the Visual Studio menu bar, click **Debug, Start Without Debugging** and enter two numbers to see the Assembly function return their sum total

```
C:\WINDOWS\system32\cmd.exe                          —    □    ✕
Enter Number: 100
Enter Another: 400
Total: 500
Press any key to continue . . .
```

```
C:\WINDOWS\system32\cmd.exe                          —    □    ✕
Enter Number: 8
Enter Another: 16
Total: 24
Press any key to continue . . .
```

175

Timing Assembly Speed

Using Assembly programs for text manipulation is tedious and better handled in a high-level language such as C++. Similarly, calling Windows functions from Assembly offers no real benefits over a high-level language, as both call the exact same library functions. Assembly's strong point is its number-crunching speed when using Streaming SIMD Extensions (SSE).

This example replicates the same operation in nested C++ loops and in an Assembly loop. It then reports the number of milliseconds taken by each operation for comparison:

SPEED
Source.asm

1 Create a new C++ **Console App** project named "SPEED", set the **Build Customizations** for MASM, then add a **Source.asm** file as usual

2 Open **Source.asm** in the Editor window and add a **.CODE** section containing a loop that will assign two received array arguments to XMM registers, then multiply each element repeatedly until a counter reaches a limit specified by a third received argument

```
.CODE
DoRun PROC
MOV RAX, 1
MOVDQA XMM1, XMMWORD PTR [RCX]
MOVDQA XMM2, XMMWORD PTR [RDX]
start:
MULPS XMM1, XMM2
INC RAX
CMP RAX, R8
JL start
RET
DoRun ENDP
END
```

SPEED
SPEED.cpp

3 Open the **SPEED.cpp** file in the Editor window, then add some inclusions and embed the Assembly function

```
#include <iostream>
#include <chrono>

using namespace std ;
using namespace std::chrono ;

extern "C" int DoRun( float*, float*, int ) ;
```

4 Add a **main** function that begins by declaring variables for arithmetic and speed measurement

```
int main( ) {
  float arr[64] = { 1.00000f, 2.00000f, 3.00000f, 4.00000f } ;
  float mul[64] = { 1.00002f, 1.00002f, 1.00001f, 1.00001f } ;
  const int million = 1000000 ;

  steady_clock::time_point t1, t2 ;
  duration<double, milli> span ;
```

5 Next, add nested loops that perform arithmetic then output the duration of the operation

```
  t1 = steady_clock::now( ) ;
  for ( int i = 1; i < million; i++ ) {
    for ( int j = 0; j < 4; j++ ) {
      arr[ j ] *= mul[ j ] ;
    }
  }
  t2 = steady_clock::now( ) ;
  span = t2 - t1 ;
  cout << "\n\tC++ : " << span.count( ) << " ms" << endl ;
```

6 End the main function by calling the Assembly function to perform the same arithmetic as that of the nested loops, then output the duration of the operation

```
  t1 = steady_clock::now( ) ;
  DoRun( arr, mul, million ) ;
  t2 = steady_clock::now( ) ;
  span = t2 - t1 ;
  cout << "\n\tASM : " << span.count( ) << " ms" << endl ;
  cout << "\n\t" ;
  return 0 ;
}
```

7 On the Visual Studio menu bar, click **Debug**, **Start Without Debugging** to see the speed comparison

The operation in this example multiplies each element of the first array by the value in the element of the same index number in the second array – 1 million times.

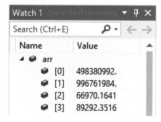

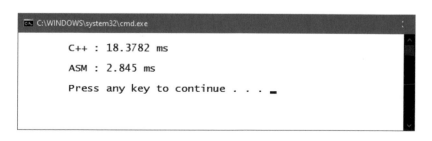

Debugging Code

Running Assembly programs in Visual Studio's Debug Mode allows the programmer to step through each line of code and observe the actions in both Watch and Registers windows. But debugging Assembly code that is external to a C++ program is more difficult because the debugger may only recognize breakpoints set in the C++ code – it may not step to breakpoints in the Assembly code.

In order to debug Assembly code that is external to a C++ program, the programmer can use Visual Studio's Disassembly window to step to breakpoints in the Assembly code. This can be used to examine the Assembly instructions generated by the C++ compiler for the nested loops in the previous example, and draw comparisons to the manual instructions in the **DoRun** function:

1 Load the previous "SPEED" example into Visual Studio, then open the **SPEED.cpp** file in the Editor window

2 Set a breakpoint on the line containing the inner nested loop, which multiplies the array element values

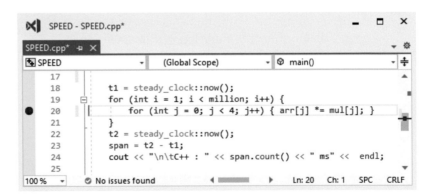

3 Next, run the code and see it stop at the breakpoint

4 On the Visual Studio menu bar, click **Debug, Windows, Disassembly** – to open a "Disassembly" window

5 Check the **Show line numbers** option, then scroll to the line containing the breakpoint

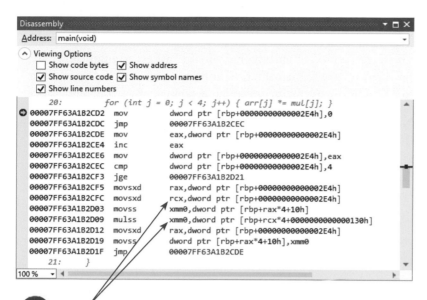

The **MOVSXD** instruction generated here moves a double word to a quad word with sign extension.

6 See that the Assembly code generated by the C++ compiler is using the **RCX** register for the inner loop counter, and the **XMM0** register for multiplication

7 Open a Watch window and add the **XMM0** and **RCX** register items

8 Click the **Step Into** button to see the generated Assembly code is performing multiplication on each individual pair of values, rather than using the full width of **XMM0**

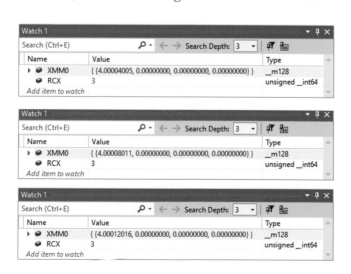

Embedding Intrinsic Code

An alternative way to gain the advantage of SIMD without writing actual Assembly instructions is provided by "intrinsics". These are C-style functions that provide access to many SSE and AVX instructions. Intrinsic functions for SSE are made available to a C++ program by including an **xmmintrin.h** header file.

Notice that the Watch window data type for the **XMM0** register in the previous example is **__m128** (two leading underscores). This is a 128-bit data type that maps to the **XMM0-XMM7** registers and can be used to initialize vectors. An assignment to a **__m128** data type is like implementing a **MOVDQA** instruction.

There are lots of intrinsic functions – those listed below perform common arithmetical operations on two **__m128** data type arguments, and return a **__m128** data type result:

Intrinsic Function	Equivalent Instruction
_mm_add_ps(*arg1, arg2* **)**	**ADDPS XMM, XMM**
_mm_sub_ps(*arg1, arg2* **)**	**SUBPS XMM, XMM**
_mm_mul_ps(*arg1, arg2* **)**	**MULPS XMM, XMM**
_mm_div_ps(*arg1, arg2* **)**	**DIVPS XMM, XMM**

INTRIN
INTRIN.cpp

1 Create a new C++ **Console App** project named "INTRIN", and open **INTRIN.cpp** in the Editor window

2 Add some inclusions, and make intrinsics available
```
#include <iostream>
#include <chrono>
#include <xmmintrin.h>

using namespace std ;
using namespace std::chrono ;
```

3 Add a **main** function that begins by declaring vectors for arithmetic and variables for speed measurement
```
int main( ) {
    __m128 v1 = { 1.00000f, 2.00000f, 3.00000f, 4.00000f } ;
    __m128 v2 = { 1.00002f, 1.00002f, 1.00001f, 1.00001f } ;

    const int million = 1000000 ;
    steady_clock::time_point t1, t2 ;
    duration<double, milli> span ;
```

4 Next, add a loop that performs multiplication arithmetic

```
t1 = steady_clock::now( ) ;
for ( int i = 1; i < million; i++ )
{
  v1 = _mm_mul_ps( v1, v2 ) ;
}
t2 = steady_clock::now( ) ;
```

5 End the main function by writing the duration of the operation using intrinsics

```
span = t2 - t1 ;
cout << "\n\tIntrinsics : " << span.count( ) << " ms" ;
cout <<  endl << "\n\t" ;
return 0 ;
}
```

6 Set a breakpoint against the line performing multiplication, then run the code and open a Watch window to see intrinsics use the full width of **XMM0**

You can find a complete list of intrinsic functions at **docs.microsoft.com/ en-us/cpp/intrinsics/ x64-amd64- intrinsics-list**

7 On the Visual Studio menu bar, click **Debug, Start Without Debugging** to see the performance speed

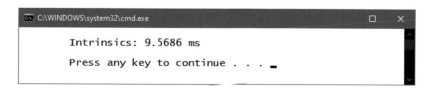

Running SSE Intrinsics

Intrinsic functions for SSE are made available to a C++ program by including an **xmmintrin.h** header file.

Notice in the Watch window that the data type for the 128-bit registers, such as **XMM0**, is **__m128** (two leading underscores). An assignment to an **__m128** data type is like implementing a **MOVDQA** instruction.

A useful SSE function **_mm_load_ps( )** (one leading underscore) can accept the name of a **float** array variable as its argument, to copy its packed single-precision values into a variable of the **__m128** data type.

This example replicates the same operation in nested C++ loops and in an Assembly loop using SSE SIMD instructions for 128-bit registers. It then reports the number of milliseconds taken by each operation for comparison:

SSESPD.cpp

1 Create a new C++ **Console App** project named "SSESPD"

2 Open the **SSESPD.cpp** file in the Editor window, then add some inclusions to make SSE intrinsics available
```
#include <iostream>
#include <chrono>
#include <xmmintrin.h>

using namespace std ;
using namespace std::chrono ;
```

3 Next, add a **main** function that begins by declaring variables for arithmetic and speed measurement
```
int main( ) {
  float arr[4] = { 1.0f, 2.0f, 3.0f, 4.0f };
  float mul[4] = { 1.000001f, 1.000002f,
                          1.000003f, 1.000004f } ;
  const int million = 1000000 ;
  steady_clock::time_point t1, t2 ;
  duration<double, milli> span ;
```

4 Add statements to initialize two variables with the values contained in the two arrays
```
  __m128 v1 = _mm_load_ps( arr ) ;
  __m128 v2 = _mm_load_ps( mul ) ;
```

...cont'd

5 Now, add nested loops that perform arithmetic then output the duration of the operation

```
cout << "\n\tFour Million Operations:" << endl;
t1 = steady_clock::now( ) ;
for ( int i = 1 ; i < million ; i++)
{
    for ( int j = 0 ; j < 4 ; j++) { arr[ j ] *= mul[ j ] ; }
}
t2 = steady_clock::now( ) ;
span = t2 - t1 ;
cout << "\n\tC++ : " << span.count( ) << << " ms" endl ;
```

6 End the main function with a loop that performs the same operation as the nested loops, but using SSE intrinsics to perform four operations on each iteration

```
t1 = steady_clock::now( ) ;
for ( int i = 1; i < million; i++)
{
  v1 =_mm_mul_ps( v1, v2 ) ;
}
t2 = steady_clock::now( ) ;
span = t2 - t1;
cout << "\n\tSSE : " << span.count( ) << " ms" << endl ;
cout << "\n\t" ;
return 0 ;
}
```

7 On the Visual Studio menu bar, click **Debug, Start Without Debugging** to see the speed comparison

```
C:\WINDOWS\system32\cmd.exe

        Four Million Operations:

        C++ : 10.2718 ms

        SSE : 4.8382 ms

        Press any key to continue . . . _
```

The result is in milliseconds (thousandths of a second), not in seconds.

Running AVX Intrinsics

Intrinsic functions for AVX are made available to a C++ program by including an **intrin.h** header file.

Notice in the Watch window that the data type for the 256-bit registers, such as **YMM0**, is **__m256** (two leading underscores). An assignment to an **__m256** data type is like implementing a **VMOVDQA** instruction.

A useful AVX function **_mm256_load_ps( )** can accept the name of a **float** array variable as its argument, to copy its packed single-precision values into a vector of the **__m256** data type.

This example replicates the same operation in nested C++ loops and in an Assembly loop using AVX SIMD instructions for 256-bit registers. It then reports the number of ticks taken by each operation for comparison:

AVXSPD.cpp

1 Create a new C++ **Console App** project named "AVXSPD"

2 Open the **AVXSPD.cpp** file in the Editor window, then add some inclusions to make AVX intrinsics available

```
#include <iostream>
#include <chrono>
#include <intrin.h>

using namespace std ;
using namespace std::chrono ;
```

3 Next, add a **main** function that begins by declaring variables for arithmetic and speed measurement

```
int main( ) {
    float arr[8] = { 1.0f, 2.0f, 3.0f, 4.0f, 5.0f, 6.0f, 7.0f, 8.0f };
    float mul[8] = { 1.000001f, 1.000002f,
                     1.000003f, 1.000004f,
                     1.000005f, 1.000006f,
                     1.000007f, 1.000008f } ;
    const int million = 1000000 ;
    steady_clock::time_point t1, t2 ;
    duration<double, milli> span ;
```

4 Add statements to initialize two vectors with the values contained in the two arrays

```
    __m256 v1 = _mm256_load_ps( arr ) ;
    __m256 v2 = _mm256_load_ps( mul ) ;
```

5 Now, add nested loops that perform arithmetic then output the duration of the operation

```
cout << "\n\tEight Million Operations:" << endl;
t1 = steady_clock::now( ) ;
for ( int i = 1 ; i < million ; i++)
{
    for ( int j = 0 ; j < 8 ; j++) { arr[ j ] *= mul[ j ] ; }
}
t2 = steady_clock::now( ) ;
span = t2 - t1 ;
cout << "\n\tC++ : " << span.count( ) << " ms" << endl ;
```

6 End the main function with a loop that performs the same operation as the nested loops, but using AVX intrinsics to perform eight operations on each iteration

```
t1 = steady_clock::now( ) ;
for ( int i = 1; i < million; i++)
{
  v1 =_mm256_mul_ps( v1, v2 ) ;
}
t2 = steady_clock::now( ) ;
span = t2 - t1;
cout << "\n\tAVX : " << span.count( ) << " ms" << endl ;
cout << "\n\t" ;
return 0 ;
}
```

7 On the Visual Studio menu bar, click **Debug**, **Start Without Debugging** to see the speed comparison

```
C:\WINDOWS\system32\cmd.exe

    Eight Million Operations:

    C++ : 20.324 ms

    AVX : 5.5947 ms

    Press any key to continue . . . _
```

Summary

- An Assembly program can be split into separate files for modularization and to make the code more manageable.

- The **EXTERN** directive can be added to the **main** program file to define external symbols, such as function names.

- The Microsoft Library Manager **lib.exe** can be used to create **.lib** library files that reference external procedures.

- The **INCLUDELIB** directive makes library functions available.

- The **PROTO** directive imports individual functions from a library into the **main** program.

- The C++ statement defining an Assembly function is specified with **extern "C"** followed by the function signature describing its return data type, function name, and any parameters.

- Arguments are passed from a C++ caller to the **RCX, RDX, R8,** and **R9** registers.

- The advantage of Assembly programming is the speed of arithmetical operations with SIMD.

- A C++ loop can perform multiple floating-point operations individually, but SSE and AVX can perform them in parallel.

- Intrinsics are C-style functions that provide access to many SSE and AVX instructions.

- Including the **xmmintrin.h** header file in a C++ program makes the SSE intrinsic functions available.

- An assignment to the 128-bit **__m128** data type is like implementing a **MOVDQA** Assembly instruction.

- The **_mm_load_ps( )** function can copy the element values from a **float** array into a variable of the **__m128** data type.

- Including the **intrin.h** header file in a C++ program makes the AVX intrinsic functions available.

- An assignment to the 256-bit **__m256** data type is like implementing a **VMOVDQA** Assembly instruction.

- The **_mm256_load_ps( )** function can copy the element values from a **float** array into a variable of the **__m128** data type.

Index

S